TO HASLEMERE
& LONDON
DUKE OF
CUMBERLAND
A286
LODSWORTH
LANGHAMS
EASEBOURNE
WHITE HORSE
PRIORY
COWDRAY PARK
HALFWAY BRIDGE
HORSE GUARDS
A272
TO PETWORTH
COWDRAY
HOUSE
RIVER
TODHAM
TILLINGTON
SELHAM
HIGHSTANDING
SOUTH
AMBERSHAM
THREE MOLES
HOYLE FARM
THE UNICORN
HEYSHOTT
WESTERLANDS
GRAFFHAM
WHITE HORSE
SOUTH DOWNS
WOOD

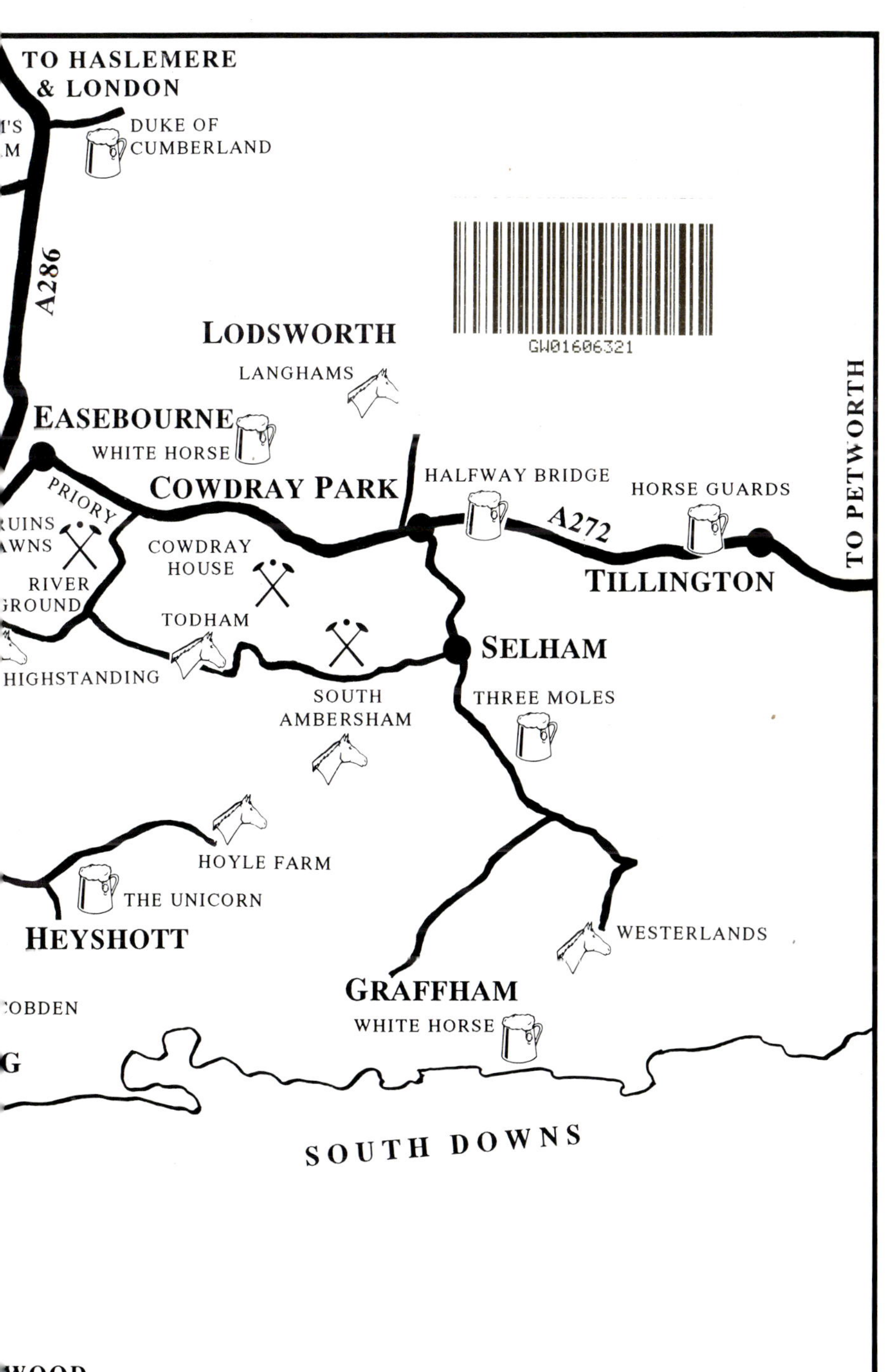

GW01606321

POLO AT COWDRAY

Spirit of Cowdray

POLO AT COWDRAY

Home of English Polo since 1910

With a Foreword by HRH The Prince of Wales

by

Derek Russell-Stoneham

&

Roger Chatterton-Newman

Polo Information Bureau

MCMXCII

To our families - for their
support and endurance

ISBN 0-9519093-0-4

British Library Cataloguing-in-Publication Data.
A catalogue record for this book is available from the British Library.

Printed in Great Britain by Acorn Press, Kings Drive, Midhurst, West Sussex GU29 0BN.

Published by the Polo Information Bureau, Citibox 35, 2 Old Brompton Road, London SW7 3DQ.

TREADING IN

In ancient China, each goal in a polo match was recorded by posting one of twenty-four flags in a frame by the steps of the imperial palace. If the Emperor's team won, the crown shouted 'Wan sui' (Long live the Emperor); if the opposition, 'Hao, hao' (Good, good). Whenever a goal was scored, the player responsible had to dismount and thank his sovereign.

We have to 'flag' a large number of people, without whom this book would have been impossible; not least, of course, Viscount Cowdray, who allowed us to contemplate it in the first place, and his sisters, the Hon Mrs John Lakin and the Hon Mrs Hugh Carter, without whose support we would have hardly scored a respectable goal in the first chukka.

Our thanks, too, to the Hon Michael Pearson and the Hon Charles Pearson, HH The Raj Mata of Jaipur, Lt Col A. F. Harper DSO, Brigadier Arthur Douglas-Nugent, polo manager at Cowdray Park, his predecessor, Peter Cruden, and assistant polo manager Sarah Sugden; Mrs Stuart Angell, who so kindly allowed us access to her late husband's notes on his long life on the Cowdray Estate; Mollie Tatham, Terry Hanlon, Peter Holman, Tony Tame, Ione O'Brien, Susan Maxwell, Mrs William Woodcock, Brenda Freeling, Brian and Annette Bethell, Paul and Sheldon Withers; Buff Crisp, secretary of the Hurlingham Polo Association, who allowed us the run of his attic; Robert Owen, Joe Plotka, Martyn Dearden, Colin Baillieu, Brook and Tim Johnson, David Jamison, Viscount Mersey, Lord Patrick Beresford, William Loyd, Editor of *Hurlingham Polo;* Lt Cmdr Robert de Pass RN, Jackie Wright, Alan Kent, Julian Hipwood, Lavinia Black, Richard Guess; Colin, Andrew, Charles and Hector Seavill; Oliver Ellis, Nicky and Lulu Evans, Major Ronnie Ferguson, Will Lucas, Charles Fraser, Sarah Dukes, Tim Fane; Alfred Clark and Michael Focard de Fontefiguires, for invaluable help with photography, and intrepid pilot Ralph Hubbard; the staff of the West Sussex County Record Office, Chichester; Johnnie Kidd; Patrick Kagan (for seasonal fortification with 'Brownies'), Peter Gilbert, Colin Emson; Michael Chevis; Bob and Michael Etherington, who so ably maintain the Cowdray polo grounds, Wendy Sutton and Phil Clarke of Acorn Press (Midhurst) and all those kind players, members and supporters of Cowdray Park Polo Club who ordered copies of the book in advance of publication. We must also thank Michael

Porter and his Winchester branch of Coutt's Bank, without whose support the book might never have received a decent handicap.

The montage on the centre pages shows a selection of 'Cowdray people' - players, members and friends, taken by Derek Russell-Stoneham over the last three seasons.

Treading in

CONTENTS

KENSINGTON PALACE

When the Second World War ended polo, as far as the game in England was concerned, faced extinction. Ponies and young players were scarce, not least because of the mechanisation of the Cavalry, the traditional training-ground for the game. Furthermore, the headquarters of the game, Hurlingham, had lost its ground as part of the war effort. A number of polo clubs were revived after the war, but it was at Cowdray Park that perhaps the most valiant attempt to revive the game took place, due to the untiring enthusiasm and hard work of Lord Cowdray and a small, but equally devoted, band of pre-war players. Ponies were found, somehow, and the opportunity provided for young and far from well-off players to play chukkas. Public interest was encouraged, far exceeding initial expectations.

In a few short years Cowdray Park had become the home of polo in the United Kingdom, and remains so. The annual British Open Championship for the Gold Cup, inaugurated at Cowdray Park in 1956, replaced the old Hurlingham Champion Cup, first played for in 1876, and its final is today the highlight of the polo year. I have been trying to win it for the past 14 years, but despite being in the final twice this particular prize has eluded me!

The Season at Cowdray Park offers spectators and players the best in low, medium and high goal polo. Young players are constantly encouraged with exposure to high goal polo and the experience of their elders, many of them of international standing; and the future of the Club, and of the game, seems assured for the 21st Century. Polo, as a sport in this country, owes an enormous amount to the enthusiasm and generosity of Lord Cowdray and I well remember his particular kindness in giving me one of his old and experienced polo ponies when I first started playing the game virtually 30 years ago. She was a kind of Maltese Cat and one of the best teachers you could have.

INTRODUCTION

by the Viscount Cowdray

I was born in the year in which my father started polo at Cowdray Park and, from the time I played my first chukka on Long Island, New York at the age of seventeen, I have been devoted to the greatest game in the world.

I am delighted that the authors of this book have attempted to tell the story of the club, from those early days, over eighty years ago, when family and friends of my parents would play weekend games on the House Ground, to the present day, when Cowdray Park is the leading British club.

The change in my lifetime has been enormous, not least in the number of players, ponies and teams involved and the greatly-extended season. In my early polo days, we played chukkas all through April, to get the ponies fit. There would be house parties here at weekends, with seventeen or more people staying, and we would all play for fun. We would go up to London on 1st May for the more serious matches at Hurlingham, Ranelagh or Roehampton.

As HRH The Prince of Wales says in his kind Foreword, after the Second World War polo was in the doldrums, and many people considered it to have no future, at least in England. The increased popularity of the game in the 1950s and later has seemed to prove them wrong and I believe that Cowdray Park has led the way, not only in reviving the sport in this country, but in spearheading its appeal to a wider audience.

The authors have recalled highlights in the developments of the club and of polo generally. They tell the stories of the Coronation Cup of 1953; of the start of the Cowdray Park Gold Cup, now the game which everyone hopes to win, in 1956 and of the many other tournaments we play here. Figures from the past are remembered: Mike Holden White and his Polo Cottage team; Hanut Singh who was as old as the century when he won the Gold Cup in 1964 and 1965; Archie David, Bunny Mathew-Lannowe, and many more come to life again for those who knew them and now for a young generation to whom they are just legends.

The economic situation will be a deciding factor in the future of polo, particularly in this age of the highly-paid professional, another change in my lifetime. But while the Army is no longer the forcing ground for young players, the excellent work of the Pony Club, and of the local patrons who recognise the potential of the 'Young Entry', should ensure that low and medium goal polo will continue in West Sussex.

The authors discovered a Press cutting in an album belonging to my sister, Daphne Lakin, which mentions the '18th century privacy'into which West Sussex retreated after Goodwood Week. That is, to a certain extent, true today, with medium and low goal matches making up what is virtually a second season once the Gold Cup final is over. Matches then take on an air more familiar to older members; the tense excitement of the Gold Cup is over; we all relax, and while the games in August and September are just as important to the teams participating, there is certainly a more intimate atmosphere, if not altogether an 18th century one.

I look forward to many more years of polo at Cowdray Park and, with luck, a Gold Cup victory for my team.

AT COWDRAY PARK DURING POLO WEEK 1927: THE HOUSE GROUND

'The polo grounds at Cowdray Park, the residence of Lord Cowdray, are among the most famous private grounds in the south of England. The Cowdray week, during which some of the best teams in the country are seen in opposition, always coincides with Goodwood, the racecourse itself being not far distant. The week which should have been held last month was abandoned, owing to the death of the late Lord Cowdray. Reading from left to right, this picture shows: Stringer, the groundsman; Major Vivian Lockett, umpiring on Heave Ho; Willie Quinnell, a stable-boy; Wyatt and Fletcher, scoring clerks (at the table); a player in Cowdray colours; Bullen, the stud-groom (seated on box); May Queen, a pony by the Best out of Eve May; and Star Shot (head and shoulders only), a hunter.' This is the original caption to a painting by Mrs Horace Colmore, exhibited at the Gieves Gallery, London, in the summer of 1927. (Courtesy of Harrison T. Hanlon).

CHUKKA ONE

The Wood of Hazels

'They disputed not . . . they disobeyed not the Queen . . .' Sir Anthony Browne, 1st Viscount Montague of Cowdray (d. 1592)

Although John la Coudraye is recorded as early as 1279, the first mention of Cowdray (from the Old French, coudraie, or hazel copse) as a place appears in an inquisition of 1284/5. Its original name was Sengle, from the Saxon for brushwood thicket, transformed gradually by rustic tongues into Single Park, a name still known in 1529.

The ruins of Cowdray House - it was never a castle, despite popular appellation - which today form so dramatic a backdrop for games of polo on the Lawns and River grounds, stand on an ancient site. The Bohun family, lords of Midhurst from time to time of Henry I until 1492, lived originally in a castle on St Anne's Hill, east of Midhurst church and commanding both the town and the parkland bounded by the Western Rother. The river, which gives a name to the favourite ground of polo players, rises some nine miles west-north-west of Cowdray, on the Hampshire-West Sussex border at Rake; and, like Cowdray, was a name unknown to the Saxon settlers who called it the Shyre, or Scyre, meaning 'bright', and thus it remained until the early 15th century.

The Rother flows on to join the Arun at Hardham, beyond Pulborough; but here one of the Bohun family utilised it to form a moat round the site of his new house of La Coudraye towards the end of the 13th century. The move from the castle to the park suggests peace and tranquility in the Midhurst of the Middle Ages, although in 1320 Joan, Lady de Bohun, complained that the 'new' house had been broken into and £3,000 worth of damage caused*. It was a staggering figure for those days: infuriatingly, further details of the attack, if such it was, have been lost.

The house now in ruins replaced Lady de Bohun's La Coudraye. The eventual heiress of the Bohun family, Mary, married Sir David Owen, sup-

* Calendar of Patent Rolls 1317-21, p.539.

posedly an illegitimate son of Owen Tudor and thus uncle of Henry VII; and it was Sir David who began work on Cowdray House about 1520. He had only a life interest in the property, and although he remained at Cowdray until his death in 1535 the estate was sold by his son, Sir Henry Owen, to Sir William Fitzwilliam KG in 1529. Fitzwilliam, who paid £2,193 6s 8d for Cowdray, was a favourite of Henry VIII and had once been his whipping-boy, taking the punishments deserved by the young prince. Treasurer of the King's Household, Lord High Admiral and Lord Privy Seal, he moved into Cowdray when David Owen was buried beneath an alabaster effigy in the former priory church of Easebourne, at the gate of Cowdray Park.

Fitzwilliam was created Earl of Southampton in 1537, shortly after receiving the dissolved Easebourne Priory from the king. Here lies one origin of the so-called Cowdray Curse, with the last sub-prioress calling down Heaven's 'curse of fire and water' on the Earl of Southampton and his family. By coincidence the earl's half-brother and heir, Sir Anthony Browne was similarly cursed in 1538 when taking possession of Battle Abbey, near Hastings: ' . . . by fire and water thy line shall come to an end and perish out of the land . . .'

That the curse did not take effect for over two centuries makes one suspect that it was concocted at a later date, increasing the drama in local eyes of the tragic end of Cowdray House and the Browne family. Unfortunately, it was well-known locally long before Cowdray burned in 1793, although coincidence was probably a word not much used in Midhurst of the 18th century. The tale fits in well with the popular image of dispossessed nuns and monks thrown out into the world by a mercenary king; and while the Dissolution did cause hardship among countryfolk who, for centuries, had found succour and relief in illness and old age within monastery gates, the closure of Easebourne Priory appears to have been long overdue. As early as 1440, Prioress Elizabeth had been reprimanded for her extravagant lifestyle. The Bishop of Chichester ordered her to be 'rightly content' with four horses and to sell her 'choice dress' to help discharge the priory's debts. Not long before dissolution, complaints were made about the unseemly behaviour of the nuns, described illuminatingly as 'wild females, scions of high family, put there to keep them quiet'. Presumably they were returned to those, perhaps unwilling, families.

As far as Battle is concerned, the picture of destitute monks is wholly inaccurate. Far from being left to fend for themselves, all received pensions: Abbot John Hammond received one worth £100 a year, a considerable sum then; Prior Richard Salehurst £10 and the other brethren £6 or more each. The former abbot continued to live at Battle and was buried in the parish church in 1546; and several of the monks became beneficed clergy, as was the case throughout England.

Accursed or not, the Earl of Southampton continued building work at Cowdray and, as a recent historian has written*, the house was a splendid achievement:

The great hall was lighted by windows on one side, and at the upper end was a life-sized carved wooden buck holding a shield with the arms of England . . . Ten other bucks, large as life, were standing, lying or sitting elsewhere. A magnificent stairway led to the great chamber, and a massive gatehouse of three storeys with turrets at each corner provided the only feature reflecting the character of a castle. The house was built round a quadrangle, its walls filled with rubble imported from the Low Countries in exchange for wood. The great windows and many inside features were in the tradition of the Renaissance . . .

The porch in the east range retains the royal coat of arms, erected to commemorate a visit by Henry VIII in 1538, and the ceiling bears the Tudor rose, the Prince of Wales's feathers, Lord Southampton's initials; anchors, recalling his post as Lord High Admiral and two heads, perhaps representing the earl and his wife.

The life-sized bucks were installed by Sir Anthony Browne, Southampton's half-brother who inherited Cowdray when the earl was killed campaigning against the Scots in 1542. The previous year had seen the arrival at Cowdray of Margaret, Countess of Salisbury, an unwilling visitor who came here for interrogation before being escorted to the Tower of London, where she lost her head at the age of sixty-nine. The last of the Plantagenets, her judicial murder by her cousin, Henry VIII, was caused not by her refusal to eschew her Faith but by her kinship with the House of York. It was the first of many blots on Henry Tudor's record.

Sir Anthony Browne's career was summarised on his portrait, once in the chapel at Cowdray and now in the Royal Collection, Hampton Court: 'He, living, was all at one time and to his death, Master of the Horse to King Henry VIII and afterwards to King Edward VI, Captain of both their

Doris Gundry, *Midhurst Yesterday and Today* (Pulborough, 1984).

majesties' gentlemen pensioners, Chief Standard Bearer of Ireland, justice in eyre of all their forests, parks and chases beyond the river of Trent northward lieutenant of the forest of Windsor, Wolmar (now Woolmer, a remnant of the Saxon Andredsweald to the north-east of Midhurst) and Ashdown, with divers parks and chases southward, one of the executors of King Henry VIII, one of the most noble Order of the Garter.'

Browne's appointment as Master of the Horse, in 1539 and at an initial salary of £40 a year, is in retrospect highly appropriate for an owner of Cowdray which, four centuries later, was to become home to the fastest sport in the world involving horses. Suitably, too, that eventual successor to Browne, the 3rd Viscount Cowdray, was to appoint his own Master of the Horse.

Browne, in his short tenure at Cowdray, can have spent a little time there. He had estates at Byfleet, Surrey, and at Battle where he started to build a new mansion. Described as one of the most energetic, influential courtiers of the 16th century, he succeeded in retaining the favour of his

Beryl, Lady Cowdray (centre) serves tea during Goodwood Week before the war

despotic royal master. The king's reception of his fourth wife, Anne of Cleves, is well known: one longs for Browne's opinion of the homely German princess, for he was sent to Cleves as proxy bridegroom. His leg was arrayed in white satin 'for the purpose of being thrust into the bed of the princess, in token of the real husband's rights over his wife . . .'

In 1544 he accompanied the king to the Siege of Boulogne and commissioned paintings of events in the French campaign. Like so much more, they were lost in the Cowdray fire of 1793 but, fortunately, five years earliver the artist S.H. Grimm, who sketched widely in the Midhurst area*, engraved copies for the Society of Antiquaries of London, in whose possession they remain.

Browne was given the unenviable task of telling Henry VIII that his end was approaching - and received £300 in the king's will, as well as being appointed a guardian of the new king, Edward VI, and his sister, the future Elizabeth I.

Polo on the Lawns in front of Cowdray Ruins

Browne and his son and namesake, created Viscount Montague by Philip and Mary in 1554, are indeed admirable studies in diplomacy, tact and loyalty - to their church, as well as their sovereign. Apart from a lapse in the late 18th century**, the Montagues remained staunch Roman Catholics, and it was the first viscount who defended the loyalty of Midhurst Catholics in Elizabeth's reign with the memorable words: 'It was known to all men that (they) had created no disturbance in the realm. They disputed not; they preached not; they disobeyed not the Queen.'

*Grimm seems to have come to this part of the country at the invitation of the Revd Gilbert White (1720-93) of Selborne, whose Natural History of Selborne was to appear, illustrated by Grimm, in 1789. His enchanting sketches include many of the churches in the Midhurst area.
**Frances, wife of the 7th Viscount, persuaded her husband to become a Protestant, although he returned to the Catholic Church before he died. She lived until 1814, having seen the destruction of the house and the extinction of the male line.

In a day of turncoats, the royal respect accorded Sir Anthony Browne obviously served his son well and both Edward VI and Elizabeth were to be guests at Cowdray. Edward was there in the summer of 1549 and wrote to his friend Barnaby Fitzpatricke (who, like Lord Southampton, had served as royal whipping-boy) of 'Cowdray, a goodly house . . . where we were marvellously, nay, rather excessively banketted . . .'

In 1588 the Spanish Armada threatened England and beacons were prepared at high points along the South Downs, which are so integral a part of the Cowdray landscape. The loyalty of Catholics was often in doubt but Lord Montague was foremost in offering his services to the Queen, as the Spanish ambassador, Mendoza, noted after the review of English troops summoned to Tilbury.

The tomb of the 1st Viscount Montague in Easebourne Church

The first that showed his bands to the Queen was that noble, virtuous, honorable man, the Viscount Montague, who now came, though he was very sickly and in age, with a full resolution to live and die in defence of the Queen and of his country against all invaders, whether it were pope, king or potentate whatsoever; and, in that ground, he would hazard his life, his children, his lands, and goods. And to show his mind agreeably thereto, he came personally himself to the Queen, with his band of horsemen, being almost two hundred; the same being led by his own sons; and with them a young child very comely, seated on horseback, being the heir of his house, that is, the eldest son to his son and heir; a matter much noted of many, whom I heard to commend the same, to see a grandfather, father and son at one time on horseback afore a queen for her service.

Elizabeth came to Cowdray for nearly a week in 1591, an event long recalled in Midhurst history and celebrated in the autumn of 1991 with a pageant. She was entertained even more lavishly than her brother and two stories have been handed down to make actors on that 16th century stage very real to us. As the queen arrived at the house, to be presented with a golden key, old Lady Montague fell upon the royal bosom, weeping and crying: 'O,happy time! O, joyful day!' Later, Mabel, Countess of Kildare, widowed sister of Lord Montague, forgot herself to the extent that she joined in with a crossbow to shoot at a herd of deer driven across Cowdray Park for royal sport. Elizabeth was, like her eventual successor on the English throne, unamused, and Lady Kildare was not a guest at dinner that day.

The first Viscount Montague died the following year and was buried in the parish church of Midhurst, his impressive monument showing the gallant old peer wearing the Garter and kneeling above the figures of his two wives and his children. In 1851 it was moved to Easebourne church, having suffered first the ravages of Cromwellian vandals and then the stupidity of Victorian builders who for six months stored it in a yard.

He was succeeded by his grandson, the 'comely child' of Tilbury, Anthony Maria Browne. Both he and his successor, Francis, 3rd Viscount Montague, were to suffer for their Faith; the former being imprisoned in the Tower of London for a year in the aftermath of the Gunpowder Plot, the latter seeing his estate sequestrated by the Cromwellians in 1644. Cowdray House was occupied by a parliamentary force under Sir William Waller and troops remained there 'to awe the Papists and malignants with which (Midhurst) is much infested and infected', until the Restoration in 1660. Francis Montague lived, for a time at least, at Stedham Hall, a small 16th century property in a neighbouring village (and where, during the summer of 1990, polo was played for the first time by Cowdray Gold Cup teams on land owned by Australian polo enthusiast Kerry Packer).

The Brownes' loyalty, and the temporary loss of Cowdray, cost them dear. Estates in Surrey were sold after the Restoration, and Battle Abbey, that alleged root of the 'Curse', went during the lifetime of Anthony, 6th Viscount, in 1719. It was this Anthony who carried out many improvements to Cowdray, and it was during his time that Samuel Johnson and Horace Walpole were, at different periods, visitors to the house in much the same way we inspect National Trust properties today.

Johnson was impressed. 'Sir', he said, during an excursion from Brighton, 'I should like to stay here four-and-twenty hours. We see how our ancestors lived.' Walpole, who found the miry roads and isolation of Sussex a 'great damper of curiosity', was 'charmed with the front, and the court, and the fountain, but the room called Holbein's, except the curiosity of it, is wretchedly painted, and infinitely inferior to . . . the private apartments at Windsor'.

Cowdray fell into a dream for most of the 18th century, to be awakened rudely on the night of 24th September, 1793. George, 8th Viscount Montague, who had inherited the estate in 1787, at the age of eighteen, had gone to the Continent with a friend, Charles Sedley Burdett, Montague was engaged to a daughter of Thomas Coutts, the banker - her sister was the following year to marry Charles Burdett's brother- and in his absence Cowdray was undergoing a major repair in preparation for the wedding. The workmen had set up their quarters in a tower above the North Gallery where, with criminal recklessness they used a charcoal brasier in a room strewn with wood shavings and other debris. At about midnight, the housekeeper, Mrs Chambers, woke to the night watchman's cry of 'Fire in the North Gallery!' The flames spread quickly, catching the wall hangings, panelling and beams, and fuelled by the pictures and furniture stored in the Gallery by the builders.

One story tells that the key to the round house in the park, now the home of the custodian of the ruins but then housing the fire engine, could not be found; and an order to break down the walls of the North Gallery was foiled by the thickness of the masonry. As the townspeople of Midhurst battled to save furniture elsewhere in the house, the inferno progressed through the building. Among the treasures lost was said to have been the original Roll of Battle Abbey, that table of the Conqueror's companions. Doubts have been cast on its existence, but the fire enabled several 19th century families to claim Norman descent unopposed.

The Dowager Lady Montague was staying at Brighton, from where she wrote a heart-rending letter to Lady Newburgh, who lived at Slindon, south-east of Midhurst.

O my dear Lady Newburgh, I am very little able to thank You as I wish and as You deserve for Your uncommon Kindness to me and my Daughter. I can't express what I feel, but must leave it to ye feelings of yr own Heart, wch I'm sure will be Your best Reward for the Obligations You bestow. I hope to accept your very kind offer, but at present yr House, wch I prefer to any other, is too near ye Scene of all my distress, and I do feel quite a Dislike to seeing any of ye people who are at Cowdray. I must blame Higgeson, for I hear it was his men who left ye Fire in ye Shavings in ye Work room. It seems a scene of Carelessness, or how could Such a House have been so destroy'd. O I ought not to look at Second Causes, the first had Doom'd it to Destruction; and I wish to submit to ye Decrees of Providence. However hard they seem they are not more than I am conscious I deserve. Bessy (her daughter) is much affected, but she feels with me yr great Kindness. Mr Sergent has just called, and put us in mind that if ye lead of ye House, wch must be worth fifteen hundred or two thousand pounds, is not saved it will be stole. So I am inclined to send a man over, as I'm sure ye Care of ye people there is not to be depended upon. A quantity of Water all round ye House, and yet it was not so employ'd as to save it. But I shall feel angry and that is sinful, so I will only return to ye pleasing fact of your kindness, and say that we hope to profit by it before we go to Town, and believe me with every sense of Gratitude, your much obliged, affectionate, etc, etc,

F.M.

Mr Sargent - John Sargent, who had lately rebuilt Lavington House, now Seaford College, near Petworth - was correct about the lead. It seems also that Lady Montague's estimation of her servants was not misplaced: there is a tradition that on the night of the fire many of them were too drunk to form a chain-gang of buckets from the Rother to the house.

A messenger was sent to Germany with the news. Alas, he was misdirected to Lausanne, rather than Lucerne, arriving at Lord Montague's lodgings an hour too late. Montague and Burdett had left to shoot the rapids at Schaffhausen on the Rhine, and are said to have built a boat specially for the purpose, despite attempts by the locals to dissuade them. At the moment the message of the fire reached the inn, the Cowdray 'curse' came into force in its second act.

The two young men entered the boat 'with a large black dog', according to the statement of an eyewitness. Dickinson, George Montague's valet, tried to restrain him, but the boat pushed off, leaving Dickinson holding his master's neckcloth and part of his collar.

They passed the bridge down the Laufen. At the first great surge the gentleman who was foremost in the boat fell or jumped into the Rhine; the boat was upset at the second wave of the Laufen, and the person who had remained in the boat swam with his companion, one after the other, through the Laufen, sometimes visible, sometimes concealed from view, and their dog with them. They were last seen swimming at the spot called Oalberg and there, in the so-called straight, they disappeared into a vortex or eddy, and were never seen again, nor were their bodies recovered. At this strait of the channel of the Rhine the river has a great depth, more than 100ft. The banks were crowded with spectators, but nobody could save the Englishmen, who swam together, endeavouring, as it appeared, to lay hold of the boat that was upset and floating along the current. They could not reach it. They sank exhausted in the whirlpool, and their dog with them.

George Montague's body was eventually recovered and buried in a local churchyard. Had the message from Cowdray not been delayed it is thought certain that he would have returned home immediately. Ironically, he and Burdett had stayed at the Eagle Inn, Laufenburg, a hostelry bearing Montague's family crest. Cowdray inherited by Montague's sister, Elizabeth, who the following year married William Stephen Poyntz, from an old Gloucestershire family, who was to sit as Whig MP for the old borough of Midhurst. The ruins were left to the jackdaws and the souvenir-seeker, while Cowdray Lodge, a mile across the park and previously occupied by a keeper, was rebuilt as the Poyntzs' home. With them lived Elizabeth's mother, Frances, Dowager Lady Montague, who died in 1814. The following year showed the tragedy had not yet been played out.

In the summer of 1815 the Poyntz family holidayed at Bognor on the Sussex coast. On 7th July, a calm and sunny day, Mr Poyntz went on a boating trip with his sons, 14-year-old William and 10-year-old Courtney, together with two friends, the Misses Parry, and the boys' tutor. The boatman had also taken out his own young son.

Two of the Poyntz daughters remained behind, but had gone down to the beach to see the boat off, and Courtney handed them a locket, which he always wore, asking them to keep it safe until he returned.

Elizabeth Poyntz and her daughters sat in the window of their lodgings, watching the boat. All was well until the middle of the afternoon when, without warning, a squall blew up and the vessel overturned. Only Poyntz and the boatman were saved. Poyntz had for a time managed to cling to the upturned boat, the boys to him, but in vain. Small wonder that talk of the curse was common in Midhurst at the time.

Mrs Poyntz died in 1830, her husband ten years later, and both were buried at Easebourne. Earlier, William Cobbett, that bombastic old journalist, had visited Cowdray' . . . to see the ruins of that once noble mansion. We entered the Park through the great iron gateway part of which being wanting, the gap was stopped up by a hurdle. We rode down to the house and all round about and in amongst the ruins, now in part covered with ivy and inhabited by innumerable starlings and jackdaws . . .'

The heirs were three Poyntz daughters, Lady Seymour, Mrs Spencer and the Marchioness of Exeter. Lady Seymour was devoted to Cowdray and would have bought out her sisters, had she the money. To solve problems over dividing the estate, Cowdray was sold in 1843 to George Perceval, 6th Earl of Egmont, for £300,000, and four centuries of family history came to an end. Apparently, a much larger sum could have been realised if the three sisters would have agreed to sell separately a part of the estate; but they refused to dismember the property.

Lord Egmont (1794-1874) was a retired Naval officer who had distinguished himself at the Battle of Navarino. He was a nephew of Spencer Perceval, who made tragic history in 1812 as the only British prime minister to be assassinated, and he already had extensive estates in Surrey and in Co Cork.

Lord Egmont seems to have made little improvement at Cowdray. The Montague Arms Inn at the top of North Street, Midhurst's main thoroughfare, became the Egmont Arms; but it was the 7th Earl, who died in 1897, who pulled down much of the old Cowdray Lodge and rebuilt it on a much larger scale: 'jolly, unpompous Victorian', as the architectural historian, Pevsner, has termed the result. The stables at Cowdray House, as the Lodge now became known, were built at the same time; although polo players on the Lawns and River grounds still use the 18th century stable block beside the ruins, built by the 6th Viscount Montague and evoking the courtyard of a French *manoir,* rather than the old grandeur of Cowdray House*.

A new era dawned at Cowdray in 1909 when the 8th Earl of Egmont

*A frew scant relics of the fire are preserved today in a small museum at the top of the Kitchen Tower, the only part of the original house to survive the blaze. The tower would also make an ideal museum of polo, a suggestion to be taken seriously, perhaps.

sold the estate to Sir Weetman Dickinson Pearson, Bt, MP for Colchester, for £340,000, only £40 more than the original Egmont purchase price. Pearson was a distinguished civil engineer and head of the construction company, S. Pearson and Son Ltd, founded by his grandfather in 1844. After a short apprenticeship, and with hardly any technical training, the 19-year-old Weetman became a partner in the company. Deciding to expand its sphere of activity, he travelled to Spain and the USA, negotiating a number of important contracts. The firm prospered and in 1884 he moved the headquarters from Bradford to London. Five years later, at the age of thirty-three, he began his long association with Mexico, gaining the friendship of the president, Porfirio Diaz. His many works there included the Mexican Grand Canal and his discovery of oil, and pioneering of the use of pipelines to fill oil tankers at sea, gave him unprecedented authority in the hitherto impoverished republic. It was only after the Great War that he relinquished his controlling interest in the Mexican oil fields to the Royal Dutch Shell Group.

River tunnels for the Pennsylvania railway, the Blue Nile Dam above Khartoum; Dover Harbour and the Blackwall Tunnel were among his other projects; and it was during the opening ceremony of the Blackwall Tunnel that Pearson was created a baronet, at the age of thirty-eight, in 1894.

But it was surely his achievements in Mexico that caught the public imagination: indeed he earned the sobriquet, 'Member for Mexico', and one biographer tells the story that Pearson was once offered the throne of Albania, his prospective subjects hoping that he could help them to economic prosperity, as he had helped Mexico*.

Unlike the hapless King Zog, Pearson resisted the temptation of a crown and in time England was to benefit from his work, during the last years of the Great War, as president of the Air Board. His duty was to consider how the air forces could be brought under a single ministry, and how the supply of aircraft could be increased; and the effectiveness of the embryo Royal Air Force owes much to his work. In 1918 he was to contribute £100,000 for the endowment of the Royal Air Force Club and, later, another substantial sum to the force's memorial fund.

Surprisingly, as *The Times* was to note in his obituary, he would emphasise in later life 'the necessity of a contractor having an expert's

*He is also remembered in Mexico today for his endowment - to the tune of £130,000 - of the Cowdray Hospital in 1918. Standing on the outskirts of Mexico City, it was opened in 1923.

knowledge of every detail of the work which he undertook . . . a praiseworthy maxim to which he himself had proved a striking exception.'

Pearson was far from being the self-made man, as has been alleged elsewhere: he made a well-established family company hugely successful, even if his engineering accomplishments tend to be overshadowed by his good fortune in the Mexican oil fields, where one well along, the Polvero, yielded a hunded thousand barrels of oil a day.

The Mexican connection is a happy one, bearing in mind that, today, high-goal polo tournaments at Cowdray include the two 10-handicap brothers, Carlos and Memo Gracida, the third generation of their family to play there.

The arrival of Sir Weetman and Lady Pearson was recalled by Stuart Angell, who came to live on the estate at the age of five in 1905, his father having been appointed foreman in the building department. Angell, himself to become a long-serving employee at Cowdray, wrote:

A large wooden arch was made to stretch from one side of the Park Gates to the other, with the words painted on in large letters, 'Welcome to Cowdray'. My father was appointed to welcome them at the gates and made a short speech and then presented to Sir Weetman and Lady Pearson an illuminated address . . . The open carriage was pulled with white ropes by some of the Estate employees, the whole of the village (Easebourne) assembled at the end of the chestnut avenue, both sides of the road . . . On arrival at the gate the carriage was stopped, Mr Aman (the agent) stepped forward and made the formal welcome . . . then came father's turn to do his bit, which he did very well . . . and everybody cheered and sang 'For he's a jolly good fellow'. Sir Weetman replied to the welcome and the men continued up the hill towing the new owners to Cowdray House.

Pearson was made Baron Cowdray in 1910 and advanced to Viscount seven years later. At one stage he considered building a new Cowdray House at the opposite end of the park to the ruins, but contented himself with adding a new wing on the north side of the Egmonts' house and generally improving and modernising the property. Between 1909 and 1914 he engaged Sir Aston Webb, the architect, to preserve the ruins, which had been fenced and ignored by the Egmonts.

It was the new owner's eldest son, Harold who was to pave the way for Cowdray's place in the history of polo. Shortly before his father bought Cowdray, Harold had married Beryl Spencer-Churchill, a grand-daughter of the 6th Duke of Marlborough and, in due course, moved to Capron House in the attractive old Cowdray Ruins. Capron House, later presented by the family to the adjoining Midhurst Grammar School as the headmas-

The 2nd Lord Cowdray and his family about 1929

ter's house, was named after an earlier owner, Anthony Capron, who had acquired a considerable estate in the area towards the end of the 17th century.

Now, it was to give its name to the first polo team set up by Harold Pearson in 1910*.

*Appropriately, the new Mrs Pearson came from a family that had helped to preserve a relic of the original Cowdray House. From 1791 to 1831, Lord Robert Spencer, a son of the 3rd Duke of Marlborough, lived at Woolbeding, up river from Midhurst. After the fire a copy (or, as some said, the original) of a fountain in the central courtyard of the ruined house was re-erected at Woolbeding. The 6th Duke, who died in 1857, inherited from Lord Robert the delightfully-named Manor of Didlinges-Dumpford, some six miles west of Midhurst. It was sold after his death.

I well remember the team (wrote Stuart Angell): the Hon Harold Pearson and Clive Pearson, Mr Clive Burns, Major Harrison as Back, also Major Ashton, Col Lockett, Capt Walford, Mr Milburn, Mr Guest, Lord Dalmeny . . . some of the players were 8, 9 and 10 handicap. What a crowd attended the games - it was mostly horse traffic, a few cars and a great number of pedestrians, a lot walking in from the surrounding villages. No one was refused admission, which was free, or tea if they wanted it . . .

The first polo match in England had been played in 1869, the 10th Hussars, based at Hounslow, taking on the 9th Lancers. By 1872 international contests were being held, with Hurlingham taking up the game - as an additional attraction to pigeon shooting - a year later. Development was rapid, with clubs being formed at Cambridge University (1873) and Oxford (1878) and private clubs led by the Monmouthsire, which played its first match in 1872. Ranelagh became the second London club in 1878, to be followed by Wimbledon; and the pattern was the same overseas, polo being played in every sphere of British influence. James Gordon Bennett, proprietor of the *New York Herald,* returned to the USA from an English visit in 1876, complete with a supply of sticks and balls; and Harry Blasson, a New York riding master, was sent to Texas to buy serviceable ponies. Within three months Westchester Polo club had been established, followed in 1881 by Meadow Brook, 'the Hurlingham of the USA'. In Latin America, Argentinian cattle ranchers took up the game in the 1870s, although the Flores Club on the edge of Buenos Aires, was not founded until 1883. The Malta Club started in 1874 and polo reached the Antipodes in 1876.

As far as England (and, therefore, the Empire) was concerned, the Army was the breeding ground for polo players, and remained so until mechanization of the Cavalry. It had been British soldiers, together with tea and indigo planters, who formed the first polo club, the Silchar, in Cachar, north-east India in 1859, playing against the Manipuris on the borders of Burma and Assam.

Strangely, there was no official polo association in India until 1892, while in England Hurlingham had quickly become the regulatory body, supported by the County Polo Association. The CPA, now amalgamated with the Hurlingham Polo Association, enabled more expert players to compete against other clubs and in the 1890s Hurlingham invited country clubs to compete for the County Cup every year in July.

Polo was certainly the most enduring of the myriad aspects of the

Indian sub-continent to capture the British imagination. The oldest recorded game in the world, it was played between the Persians and Turkomans about 600BC, according to the Persian poet, Abu'l Kasim Mansur (AD940-1020), known as Firdausi who describes a match in his so-called 'Iliad of Persia', *Shah-nama*. At Ispahan, capital of Persia until 1796, there are ruins of an ancient polo ground with stone goal posts eight yards apart and the ground three hundred yards long: the exact measurements of a modern polo ground.

Harold, Viscount Cowdray, founder of the club, and Lady Cowdray

Harold Pearson, born in 1882, started to play polo at Oxford in 1900 and was in the university team in 1903, 1904 and, as captain, 1905. Liberal MP for Eye, Suffolk, from 1906 to 1918 (at one time he and his father sat in the Commons together), he represented the House of Commons against a House of Lords team in the Harrington Cup match at Ranelagh in 1907, 1911 and 1914; and in 1911 his Capron House team won both the Novices and Points cup matches at Ranelagh.

At Cowdray he laid out the House Ground, in front of the new Cowdray House, augmenting it eventually with the Lawns and River grounds. The House Ground is today the second oldest polo ground in the country: Cirencester's Ivy Ground, first played in 1894, heads the list and the House Ground, natal place of polo at Cowdray Park, is now usually reserved for chukkas. It also sees the final of the Park House Cup, played on invitation for those not involved in the British Open Championship for the Gold Cup. It is the South Downs, Kipling's 'blunt, bow-headed, whale-backed Downs', rather than Cowdray ruins, which provide the backdrop for the House Ground; and in many ways matches there epitomise the friendly spirit of Cowdray polo, unchanged for eight decades.

In 1910, indeed for the next twenty years, polo at Cowdray Park was very much an affair for the family and friends of Harold Pearson and his brother, Clive (later to restore the magnificent Elizabethan house of Parham, near Pulborough). Enthusiastic horsemen - they founded the Cowdray Hunt together in 1922 - the impracticability of neck reins prevented them using their hunters for polo; but polo ponies, height fixed at 14.2

hands in 1895, were not yet in short supply. Indeed, in the early years of the century it was estimated that ten thousand polo ponies were stabled in the vicinity of Greater London, and this despite the closure of the Wimbledon Club in the '90s, as being too far away from London. Its successor, Roehampton, might have been supposed equally remote from the city, yet it survived until 1955.

Originally, polo was played at Cowdray only during Goodwood Week, then far more of a social occasion than today. Stuart Angell, as a schoolboy before the Great War, recalled late afternoon and early evening matches.

Lady Cowdray used to invite all the village each day and give the mothers a free tea, and the children buns and oranges, and on the Saturday when the Finals were played, mothers and fathers and children were invited to tea . . . Most of the competing teams were Army ones, the Capron House team was then the local representative. There were more high handicap players to choose from in those days as most of the Army units spent a lot of time in India . . .

As early as 1910 Harold Pearson had a handicap of 5 (his brother, Clive, was then a 3) and during Goodwood Week every year he invited teams to compete for the Cowdray Park Challenge Cup. That deceptively halcyon summer of 1914 saw ten teams enter the tournament between 27th July and 1st August, in the first round Capron House beating Petworth 13-5. Petworth, which had been raised by Capt the Hon Edward Wyndham, later the 5th Lord Leconfield, whose family owned the neighbouring Petworth estate, had received a start of 5.

Capron House (23)	Petworth (18)
1. Hon Harold Pearson	1. Capt Hon A.F. Stanley
2. Hon Clive Pearson	2. Capt Hon E.S. Wyndham
3. Capt H.C.S. Ashton	3. Major E.H. Brassey
Bk. Lt Col G.K. Angell	Bk. Capt L.H. Hardy

In the semi-final Capron House won 9-7 over the 11th Hussars (19) but lost 9-5 in the final to Cowley Manor (21). Three days later the threat of war became a reality. 'How well this is established in my mind', recalled Stuart Angell half a century later.

August 4th was a bank holiday Monday and there was always a flower show held on the bottom side of the Lawns near the Round Tower. . .

a great occasion for the village and more so this year as a polo match had been arranged; this added to the thrill of it all. During the afternoon it was announced by megaphone that we had declared war on Germany and Austria and their allies, and would all men on leave return to their units at once . . . this certainly put a damper on all our fun and activities. There were a lot of local men on a short leave . . . I witnessed a great many tearful goodbyes as people began to disperse . . .

Lord Cowdray's work at the Air Board was emulated at local level by his wife, who now converted the old refectory at Easebourne Priory into a hospital, buildings kitchens underneath. She had already endeared herself to Easebourne villagers by providing shoes and stockings for the three hundred children attending the local schools; enabling many of them to walk the long distances to and from their homes dry-shod for the first time in their lives. In the event, the hospital was never used, but at the estate yard, next door, the carpenter's shop and the sawmill were converted into dormitories for the 10th Gordon Highlanders, the harness room becomimg the quartermaster' stores.

One of the early casualties of the war was to be Lt Col G.K. Angell, commanding the 5th Dragoon Guards. A member of the Inniskilling Dragoons polo team when it won the Inter-Regimental tournaments at Hurlingham in 1897, 1898 and 1905, he had played Back in the Capron House team at Cowdray on 1st August. Another familiar figure never to return was Geoffrey Pearson, Lord Cowdray's youngest son, who in 1910 had played for Cambridge in the Inter 'Varsity match at Hurlingham, won by Oxford 10-2.

Pearson had gone to France as a motorcycle despatch rider. With his companion, who rode in the side-car, he was captured by a patrol of Uhlans; but three days later, on 6th September, 1914, the Battle of the Marne broke out and, taking advantage of a French attack, the two men attempted to escape. After crawling through long grass for five hundred yards they were nearly clear, when one of the Uhlans spotted them and opened fire: Geoffrey Pearson was killed, aged twenty-three.

Harold Pearson, who served as a major in the Sussex Yeomanry, raised at Cowdray Park, before transferring to the General Staff at Aldershot, survived the war. So, surprisingly, did a large number of polo ponies. Writing in the now-defunct *Polo Monthly* in April, 1919, the sporting parson, the Revd T.F. Dale, could say:

We are looking forward to a revival of polo. Hurlingham and Ranelagh have issued programmes for the 1919 season, nor can we doubt that there will be plenty of players - of those who played before the war there are enough left to set a standard of play and to keep up the traditions of the game. There are, I believe, more of the old stamp of polo ponies left in the country than some people seem to think.

That year saw Lord Cowdray make over the estate to Harold Pearson and, henceforth, Capron House was to be known as the Cowdray Park Polo team. It surely augured well for the future when, during the first summer of peace, a Cowdray team consisting of Harold and Clive Pearson*, Lord Stalbridge and Capt J.G. Lowther beat the 2nd Life Guards 7-2 in the final of the Roehampton Junior Championships.

The young Daphne Pearson (later Mrs John Lakin) on a polo pony for the first time

The early 'twenties were exciting years for the Cowdray park team, with victories including the Cowdray Challenge Cup of 1921, the Bordon Challenge Cup (held at a military encampment over the Hampshire border) in 1921 and 1922; the Ranelagh Open in 1922 and the Ranelagh Novices Cup in 1923. In 1923, too, Harold Pearson was elected a member of the Hurlingham Club Polo Committee, becoming chairman two years later; and it was at Hurlingham, Roehampton and Ranelagh that Cowdray Park played

*For their employees, the Pearson brothers encouraged the formation of football teams, inter-estate games being played between Cowdray Park and Clive Pearson's estates at Balcombe and Parham, as well as a team from Paddockhurst, Lord Cowdray's East Sussex home. Cricket teams were also formed, the Cowdray team eventually taking over as its changing-room the original polo changing-room opposite Cowdray ruins.

at the height of the season, having played chukkas at home during April.

Polo was played in London all through the season (recalled Stuart Angell) Cowdray Ponies going up to 10 Reeves Mews and hacking through the traffic. The teams competing for the cup during Goodwood Week all returned by train to Midhurst station. This only lasted during Goodwood Week, the finals being on the Saturday. Goodwood was a great occasion, Cowdray House was full to its limits . . . It was my job to take the lunch up to Goodwood, with four of the men staff. After I had unloaded I returned to our private car park on the north side of Trundle Hill, to see to the chauffeurs' lunch, which consisted usually of a large joint of beef, bread and cheese and jam rolls for sweet, and plenty of bottles of beer.

Goodwood Week at Cowdray in the 'twenties is also remembered with affection by Harold Pearson's fourth daughter, Brenda, now the Hon Mrs Hugh Carter:

We children would give up our rooms for guests and move to Park Cottage, now the Cowdray Park Golf Club house, with our French governess, Marmoi, who did the cooking for us . . .

Alternatively, the six Pearson children went off to Paddockhurst, near Turners Hill in East Sussex, where the first Lord Cowdray had moved after making over Cowdray Park to his son. He had bought the estate (and Dunecht in Aberdeenshire) long before Cowdray and, in 1914, had offered it as a home in exile to the deposed Porfirio Diaz of Mexico. Diaz had chosen Paris, instead.

Wherever we went, we would be summoned during Goodwood Week and come over for the most delicious fruit teas. One of my great joys was to sit on the boards - we had then in those days - on the River Ground with Daddy to watch polo. The players all seemed to be glamourous young subalterns, and I would fancy myself riding them off. I was allowed, occasionally, to play chukkas: it was the most exciting thing in the world. . .

Goodwood Week was followed by the family's annual migration to Dunecht, returning to Cowdray Park in time for the pheasant shooting. Stuart Angell, who drove luncheon out to the Guns, recalled the venison house in the estate yard being used to hang the birds, except for those needed in the house.

The rest were packed into hampers which were then taken to

Midhurst station on the Monday morning, each being labelled to a London game dealer. The Todham beat held the record for the most birds shot in one day - over 1,000. Two Guns in the party, the Quilter brothers, were both excellent shots. I saw one of them have three dead birds in the air at one time, the only time in my life I saw this happen.

Yet it is Goodwood Week that remains fixed firmly in the minds of those who came to Cowdray to watch, or to play, polo after the great War.

The teas are recalled, too, by Susan Maxwell who, as a child of twelve, came to live at The Crypt. at nearby Cocking, in the mid 1920s. Her father, Major 'Bunny' Mathew-Lannowe, late 4th Dragoon Guards, had played polo for the Tigers in India and, with a handicap of 9, for King Alfonso XIII of Spain before the Great War.

He became a great friend of Harold Cowdray and was invited to come here to help revive polo after the war. I was a contemporary of John and Angela Pearson - I shared their governess for French lessons - and I can remember the most beautiful china that Lady Cowdray would put out for tea parties in Goodwood Week.

'Bunny' Lannowe later went to run polo in Bierritz and Cannes and, in time, at Ranelagh, although he moved back to Lodsworth, beside Ambersham, in his 70s. A familiar and popular figure (as is his daughter today), he was schooling polo ponies at the age of 86.

When he was 82, Daddy said he wanted to school another pony. I was at Ascot Pony Sales one day and had just told Ryan Price the story. 'There's one going round the ring now,' he said. 'What, that one?' I said, putting my arm in the air. Of course, it was knocked down to me - this was after a good lunch - so I had to buy it. We called it 'Susan's Folly' and Fred Withers said it was a perfect pony. We had it at Ambersham and Daddy would walk over from Lodsworth to play stick and ball.

Major Lannowe died at the age of 96, working on a biography of Winston Churchill, with whom he had served in India before the turn of the century. His son-in-law, John Evans (a leading amateur rider for many years) and his grandsons, Nicky and Vivian Evans, have followed in his polo footsteps at Cowdray Park. Today, Vivian has a handicap of 2, while Nicky, who plays to a 4, was in the Guardacre team in the run-up to the 1991 Gold Cup.

Of course, when I came here (recalls their grandmother) there were no professionals: it was simply an affair of family and friends playing. But even though there is far more money involved in polo today, Cowdray has never really lost the intimate feeling I remember so well.

The Great War, far from killing off players and ponies, had only served to stimulate spectators at polo, it seems. The revival of the game after four years attracted the crowds as never before and in 1926 the finals of the Cowdray Challenge Cup were watched by three thousand people, with five or six hundred staying to tea in front of the ruins, afterwards. Horse transport was still common, of course, and older inhabitants of Midhurst and Easebourne* can recall the London cabbies coming down, starting to go through the town on the Saturday before Goodwood. They plied for hire at Singleton, Lavant and Chichester stations (all of which connected with Midhurst by one of three now-defunct lines), taking fares up to the racecourse. 'Some of the poor old horses looked as if they should have been in the knacker's yard years before,' was one comment: unlike polo ponies, the cab horses did not travel by train. Several of the cabs arrived at the polo matches before beginning the sixty-four mile journey back to London.

The first Viscount Cowdray died at the end of April, 1927, and polo was abandoned at Cowdray Park that season as a mark of respect to a well-loved Midhurst figure. The following year, however, William Woodcock began his long association with Cowdray as stud groom. Working originally in a pianoforte factory - his widow recalls how much he disliked the job - Woodcock was groom to Harold Cowdray's son and heir, John, when he went up to Oxford where he played polo with the 'Varsity team.

During Goodwood Week in particular the stables at Cowdray House would be filled with ponies, most of them arriving at nearby Selham station, on the line linking Midhurst with Victoria, or at one of the three Midhurst town stations. It was now, too, that Lord Cowdray's children began to follow in their father's footsteps in earnest. His youngest daughter, Daphne, now the Hon Mrs John Lakin, was to be rated at the height of her career as one of the best players in the country, giving the lie to the dictionary definition of polo being 'a game resembling hockey played by men on

*The two communities, divided by the Rother, have always guarded their separate identities jealously. For generations children from Easebourne would attempt to prevent Midhurst children from crossing the point on the boundary bridge marked by clasped hands. These can still be seen from the footpath opposite North Mill, by the gate to the Lawns Ground.

horseback'. In the 'twenties, of course, that accolade was some way ahead, but Daphne Lakin remembers the enthusiasm of her brother, John, his twin, Angela, born appropriately in the year in which Capron House team had been formed, and their eldest sister, Yoskyl, named after her father's favourite polo pony.

It was girls' polo in those days - we were not allowed to play with the men, and it wasn't really much fun. Angela and Yoskyl played, but my sister Nancy (now Lady Blakenham) and my Mother detested horses! My polo career started much later and I probably wouldn't have taken it up if I had not married a polo-mad husband . . .

One of the first matches recalled by Mrs Lakin took place on 3rd August, 1929, when Cowdray Park (received 5) was beaten 9-8 by the 17/21 Lancers. The home team consisted of 1. Hon W.J.C. Pearson (0), 2. Col H.C.S. Ashton (4), 3. Major R.L. Benson (4), Bk. Major J.F. Harrison (7).

In those days, or at least at that match, players wore colours on their helmets to denote their places in the team, rather than numbers on their shirts, which are so often impossible to distinguish! One was red, two white, three blue and back black. It was simple! And if a cup was won three times, the team kept the cup.

In 1931 a polo match on the River Ground was part of the celebrations for the coming of age of John Pearson and his twin, by then married to Col George Murray and mother of the future 10th Duke of Atholl. Stuart Angell remembered '. . . Tom Smith's fair* being installed at the ruins, everything was free and the celebrations were splendid . . . the weather was not; we had everything that English weather can produce in a short time .'

The same year, Lord Cowdray and his son played in a match at Hurlingham and, in 1932, were members of the Cowdray Park team which beat the 7th Hussars 5-4½ in the Bordon Tournament.

Then, in 1933, Lord Cowdray died after a short illness at the tragically young age of fifty-one. As Stuart Angell recalled: 'he was to all the employees on the estate 'Cowdray' and everything that it represented in

*More correctly, Andrew Smith, a celebrated local showman once patronised by Queen Victoria when his fair was held in Windsor High Street (or so he said). Two generations of West Sussex children knew Smith and his rusty black bowler hat.

John Pearson, later the 3rd Viscount Cowdray, prepares for a match on Long Island, New York in 1927

West Sussex. He was the real country squire. . . we had lost our best friend.'

One tale in particular summarises Harold Cowdray's character. A track leading into Knight's Copse, on the Lickfold corner of the estate, was being used for exercise by local riders, and orders went out from the estate office for them to be stopped. One Sunday morning, Lord Cowdray had ridden over to Lickfold when he was confronted at Knight's Copse by one of his woodmen, to whom he was unknown.

'Where the hell do you think you be a'going'?' asked the woodman, remembering his orders. 'Through Knight's Copse, of course,' was the reply. 'No, that you bent, not all the time I be here, so get that into your head. I've had orders not to let nobody on a horse through these 'ere woods.' Lord Cowdray's protest that he owned the property cut no ice. 'Ah, that's what they all says, and I tells you you bent going, so you may as well take your hook!' Lord Cowdray did not let on and turned back, returning to Cowdray House highly amused and pleased with the way the old man had stuck to his job. A few days later he arrived at Knight's Copse by car, with Mr Roberts, who was in charge of the estate woods department, and was introduced formally to the old woodman. 'Why, you be the gentleman that I stopped on Sunday, bent you?' 'That's right,' said Lord Cowdray, 'and you did your job well.' The old boy was flabbergasted. 'I be that sorry, sir, I

didn't know you was the boss.' 'You were only doing your job,' laughed Lord Cowdray. The old chap grabbed his hand and said, grinning all over his face, 'Good old Lordy!' This highly amused Lord Cowdray, as he had a wonderful sense of humour.

John Pearson became the third Viscount Cowdray at the age of twenty-three and soon proved himself an able successor to his father, both where the estate and polo were concerned. Six years later, polo, which had survived in the Great War unscathed, apart from the understandable abolition of the 14.2 hand regulation, was to enter its darkest period.

Cowdray ruins under snow. The fire of 1793 broke out to the right of the photograph in what was then the North Gallery

CHUKKA TWO

Home and Away

'Welcome to the Meidan, thou chief of horsemen, strike the ball!' (From a 16th century Persian polo illustration)

The new Lord Cowdray had first played polo at the age of seventeen in 1927.

I was staying at Westbury House on Long Island with Michael Phipps, an old friend of my family. When I went up to Oxford I played for four years and in my last year there - 1932- my team won the Tyro Cup, then of course a Hurlingham tournament.

To reach tournament level before the war was not always easy. John Cowdray recalls around five hundred players competing for six grounds in London, 'so unless you actually played for a team that reached a tournament, you never really got a game,'

In those days, too, rain could result in polo being cancelled at Hurlingham, Ranelagh or Roehampton for up to ten days; something which even the 1991 weather failed to accomplish at Cowdray Park. Lord Cowdray, unable to play in London, would 'phone Lord Louis Mountbatten, then at Adsdean, near Chichester, where he had laid out a Downland practice ground.

I would ask Dickie if we should bring the ponies back to Cowdray Park. If he thought we would be able to play here, we would take a special train from Barnes station to Petersfield and then be shunted back along the little branch line to Midhurst. It was much cheaper than hiring a horse box: in fact, in those days to hire a box and go by road was considered to be a great extravagance by most people. . .

Before the war, Lord Cowdray would keep about a dozen ponies at Cowdray Park, including several belonging to John Lakin, his future brother-in-law.

Lord Louis Mountbatten prepares for a pre-war match at Cowdray Park

Really, six were enough for me then, and I remember one season in London when we had to play seven match games in six days. We won them all and I still had only six ponies! I played a chukka on each and I must say that I didn't care which one I rode: they were all good. There used to be weekly auctions of polo ponies at Tattersall's in London before the war, but I think the highest price I ever paid in those days was £500 - that was from a horse coper near Midhurst - and I considered it to be expensive. At Oxford I used to buy from Jackman, a coper who would charge around £350 for a pony that was not quite finished. If it was no good, Jackman was always happy to take it back, which a lot of dealers would never do . . .

In the spring of 1939, Lord Cowdray, recently elected to the council of the Hurlingham Polo Association, went to the USA as non-playing captain of an English team hoping to regain the Westchester Cup for Great Britain. The cup, played for at Meadow Brook since 1886, when a Hurlingham team trounced the US 10-4, 14-2, had last been won by Britain in the year the previous war had broken out.

This time, however, tragedy dogged the visit. In a railway accident in

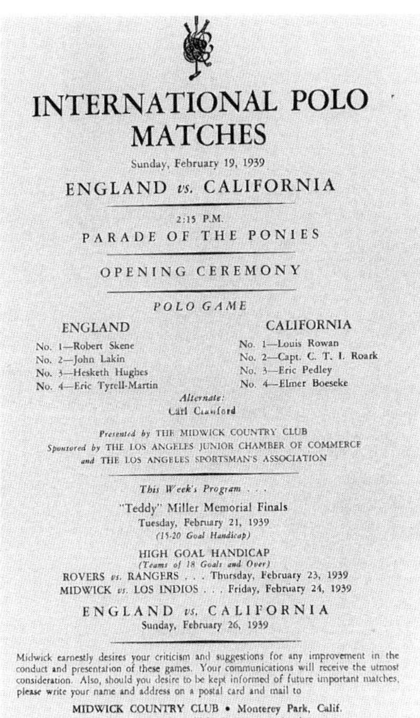

INTERNATIONAL POLO MATCHES

Sunday, February 19, 1939

ENGLAND *vs.* CALIFORNIA

2:15 P.M.

PARADE OF THE PONIES

OPENING CEREMONY

POLO GAME

ENGLAND	CALIFORNIA
No. 1—Robert Skene	No. 1—Louis Rowan
No. 2—John Lakin	No. 2—Capt. C. T. I. Roark
No. 3—Hesketh Hughes	No. 3—Eric Pedley
No. 4—Eric Tyrell-Martin	No. 4—Elmer Boeseke

Alternate:
Carl Crawford

Presented by THE MIDWICK COUNTRY CLUB
Sponsored by THE LOS ANGELES JUNIOR CHAMBER OF COMMERCE
and THE LOS ANGELES SPORTSMAN'S ASSOCIATION

This Week's Program . . .

"Teddy" Miller Memorial Finals
Tuesday, February 21, 1939
(15-20 Goal Handicap)

HIGH GOAL HANDICAP
(Teams of 18 Goals and Over)
ROVERS *vs.* RANGERS . . . Thursday, February 23, 1939
MIDWICK *vs.* LOS INDIOS . . . Friday, February 24, 1939

ENGLAND *vs.* CALIFORNIA
Sunday, February 26, 1939

Midwick earnestly desires your criticism and suggestions for any improvement in the conduct and presentation of these games. Your communications will receive the utmost consideration. Also, should you desire to be kept informed of future important matches, please write your name and address on a postal card and mail to

MIDWICK COUNTRY CLUB • Monterey Park, Calif.
Your cooperation will be greatly appreciated.

The programme for 19th February, 1939. The brilliant young British player, Capt Pat Roark, died of injuries received when his tired pony collapsed during the game at Midwick, Pasadena

Nebraska, Lord Cowdray's pony, Queen's Decision, was the only fatality out of twenty-eight mounts involved; but worse was to follow.

On 19th February the opening game was held at Midwick Country Club, Pasadena, California, the English team consisting of Robert Skene at No. 1, John Lakin at No. 2, Hesketh Hughes at No. 3 and Eric Tyrrell-Martin at Back. The captain, Gerald Balding, who had come over from India with an injured hip, had been earlier put out of action by a bad fall.

As the fourth chukka drew to a close, England was winning by 6-4. Then, riding a tired pony a minute and a half after the bell had rung supposedly to end the chukka, Capt Pat Roark, a stylish young Irish player, suffered the fall that was to cost him his life a few days later. The brother of Aidan Roark, a member of the English team, Pat had played for the team that visited the USA in 1927 and 1930, and although not chosen for the English squad in 1939 had been entered on the USA handicap lists as Britain's greatest player.

Indeed, it was obvious to observers that he would have won a place on the English team before the final of the tournament had it not been for the accident. As it was, in his last game Roark was at No. 2 for California, and his death was mourned by the international polo fraternity.

For the sake of the record, Carl Crawford took his place in the game and England won in eight chukkas by 12-7. As *Horse & Horseman* showed:

A match during the Westchester Cup final, 1939

Truly, the British challengers, who have invariably had more than their share of misfortune in international polo, have already had enough happen to them to open all hearts to them in condolence.

On 5th March, Hughes, Lakin, Skene and Tyrrell-Martin, riding in that order, met California again in a deciding match before a crowd of 7,500. This time, the Californians came from behind to win by a goal, 9-8, in the last chukka, but Pat Roark's death still overshadowed the tournament, as an editorial in *Horse & Horseman* showed:

For three years we have been consistently urging the rules committee of the various polo associations to revise their regulations, so that every period shall end on the bell, instead of continuing, as is now the custom every period of the game but the last, until the ball is hit across a boundary or the whistle blows for some reason. Polo is the only game that keeps on for indefinite periods when the bell rings . . . Seven and a half minutes at speed is plenty for a good pony; too many accidents come at the tail-end of a period when horses and men are tired and less alert than they should be. Pat Roark would be alive today if the rule we have been advocating had been passed! The fall in which this master horseman received his fatal injuries occurred when his exhausted horse crumbled after a minute and a half of overtime.

Aidan Roark, Pat's brother, also called for more protection for players and ponies. He urged that umpires be empowered to stop a game any time a pony appears in distress. 'The game should be stopped,' he wrote in a letter to the American polo Press, 'as the saving of a limb and possibly a life is surely more important than the outcome of a game which, after all, we play for pleasure.'

That the team led by Lord Cowdray played for pleasure was apparent to American polo-watchers. On 3rd April, the *San Francisco Examiner* paid a glowing tribute to the squad:

As long as polo is played, San Francisco will remember the Hurlingham riders from England who, yesterday, introduced the international brand at Golden Gate Park Bowl. The British Empire's finest horsemen swarmed, whistled, walloped and so out-classed their western United States opponents in a 15 to 7 victory that 6,000 fans gave them a standing ovation at the finish.

The British, Gerald Balding, Robert Skene, Aidan Roark and Eric Tyrrell-Martin, played the game as it was intended. They were perfect. They hit with deadly accuracy. They passed from impossible positions, straight to the receiver. Their teamwork was dazzling. And their riding was beautiful. They scored 15 goals against American aces like Cecil Smith and Eric Pedley and Elmer Boeseke. They missed another eight or ten goals by inches. More to the point was their co-ordination . . .

After the war, members of the English team were to become familiar figures on the revived home team at Cowdray Park; but for now the Westchester Cup was to prove just beyond their grasp. The Americans were to win the final by a comfortable margin, 11-7, 9-4, although as commentators noted, 'they didn't exactly drive the English off the field.'

At Cowdray Park, meanwhile, where ponies were met at Midhurst station and stabled at Cowdray House for 3s 6d a night, the polo committee was under the temporary chairmanship of Louis Mountbatten. Eight years earlier he had written, under the pseudonym 'Marco', *An Introduction to Polo,* a classic work still in print and an influence on later members of his family to play polo at Cowdray. The Cowdray Park Challenge Cup tournament in 1939 resulted in a Petworth photographer, George Garland, seeing one of his photographs appear widely in the national Press: it was of Mountbatten's sealyham dog, Topsail, guarding his master's polo sticks.

Yet even before war was declared on 3rd September, detractors of English polo were at work. Not all American commentators felt inclined to regard the visitors as worthy amateurs, and once the Westchester Cup was safe on the far side of the Atlantic it was a common saying that no English player had the skill to hit the ball as hard or as far or as straight as the Americans. The gate at Meadow Brook had also proved unsatisfactory, as did the sale of Hurlingham ponies over there. *Polo Monthly* declared that to equip and maintain a team on the 1939 scale was 'beyond the bounds of possibility for our next challenge on American soul . . . Unless some fairy godfather comes to the rescue . . .' The HPA had sponsored the team to the tune of £12,000 but there was still a deficit of £10,000.

However, more kindly, *Polo Monthly* suggested that Americans were taught the game 'from the age of 12, the British not so,' the young Englishman 'going into slow polo with little idea of what it is all about and . . . has to pick up what he knows in the hard school of trial and error. He learns with twice as much labour and sadness as does his remote relation on the other side of the Atlantic.'

Perhaps little changes: today, one hears the frequent complaint that young Englishmen are at a disadvantage, compared with their Argentinian counterparts, because young Argentinians go to school only in the morning - and play polo for the rest of the day. With the current development in independent schools' polo, this argument may soon prove falacious.

In 1939, however, the immediate future of English polo did not appear to be bleak. The year before he inherited the estate, John Pearson had formed a troop of the Sussex Yeomanry, joined by many of the younger estate workers, with Easebourne Village Institute as the section headquarters. Part of the 98th Field Brigade, the unit was equipped with 18 pounder field guns, the doors of the institute being widened to enable the guns to pass through for drill, having been manhandled from the estate yard where they were kept in a shed.

In a prelude to war, Lord Cowdray was called up as a reservist and the 506 Royal Army Service Corp took over most of Cowdray House, their vehicles parked under the avenue trees and the water supply to the estate hampered seriously by military demands. Evacuees from London arrived at Midhurst stations and, as Belgium fell, the 506 was replaced by a commando unit, some members of which were billeted on families free from evacuees.

Before that last summer of peace, the three polo grounds at Cowdray were the House, River and Lawns - the last, laid out shortly before Harold Cowdray's death. Today, of course, players and spectators are equally familiar with the grounds at Ambersham*, beyond Cowdray Park near the little village of Selham; and for years before the war ponies would arrive by train at Selham station. The quaintly named Three Moles Inn, bearing the arms of the Mitford family of nearby Pitshill, has been popular with generations of players and grooms.

In 1939, however, the flat meadows at Ambersham had not become extra polo grounds, although several players had landed on what was then a private airfield.

I made a landing ground there about 1937 (recalls Lord Cowdray). But I always though that we might end up playing polo there, so I used the right sort of grass seed . . .

On the outbreak of war, the land was taken over by the Fleet Air Arm and hangars, of which two remain on site, were built for the Walrus flying boats and Sea Otters used in sea rescue work for pilots shot down off the coast and for keeping watch on floating mines or on invasion attempts. By coincidence, as Lord Cowdray remembers:

The Sea Otters were being made by one of our family firms, Saunders Roe, on the Isle of Wight, and they asked if they could store them at Ambersham. I though that once the war was over we would be able to keep the hangars: as it happened, I had to buy them!

One wonders whether the shade of old Sir Anthony Browne, 1st Viscount Montague of Cowdray, visited the site and recalled the days of the Armada defence preparations.

At Ambersham Farm, the barn and stables (now occupied by polo ponies) became accommodation and mess for the Fleet Air Arm; while Cowdray Park was ploughed as part of the war effort, the herd of deer,

*Ambersham (from the Saxon *AEmbres ham,* or AEmbre's settlement) was for centuries an outlying portion of the distant Hampshire parish of Steep, Ambersham villagers having the right of burial at Steep. It had been settled by Jutes, who also colonised the Isle of Wight, but was granted to Ethelwalch, King of Sussex in the 7th century. Ambersham was a tithing of Steep until 1913. In 1700 the manor of Ambersham was bought by Anthony Capron, after whom Harold Cowdray's old home was named. The Caprons lived at Moor Farm, now the Cowdray home farm, and the estate was sold to W.S. Poyntz of Cowdray at the end of the 18th century.

Cowdray House, built by the Egmonts and extended by the 1st Lord Cowdray

descended perhaps from those driven before Elizabeth I for her sport, were corralled in a corner of the park. Escapes were inevitable and venison became a welcome addition to rationed diets locally. The Old House at Home, then still the Ambersham village put, welcomed the extra custom, although the landlord frequently ran out of beer, again because of rationing, and strangers were often turned away without a drink. Stuart Angell, who was in the midhurst fire crew, recalled his first call to action at Ambersham:

No hangars had yet been built there and the little brick hut had only just got the footings laid. A night bomber came in and dropped a Molotov bread basket - this consisted of dozens of incendiary bombs, opening up on release from the plane and catching fire on contact. There were small fires all over the air field, but no damage was done . . . on inspection next morning we found quite a number had not ignited and were partially buried in the soft ground. These were dealt with by the bomb disposal squad stationed at nearby Graffham.

Unlike August, 1914, there was little optimistic talk of the latest war being over by Christmas. Polo was in suspension, with the ponies turned out into the paddocks, their owners and riders in uniform. The night bombing of London began in earnest and, as Stuart Angell was to remember, 'one could have put the clocks right as the Germans came in right over us every night for weeks on end at 6.30 p.m.' Another target for the enemy planes was Tangmere fighter station, just beyond the Downs from Cowdray Park, and the Midhurst siren wailed constantly.

On nights of duty we would have our tea and then put our uniforms on, sometimes having to carry them to the fire station to finish dressing, so as to be near the 'phone for action calls. The sound of German engines was often followed by a loud explosion in the distance, or very much nearer if they were driven off by anti-aircraft fire and unloaded their bombs in their hurry to get away. We commented on the loudness of the explosions - whether it was a 250lb, 500lb or a block buster, these often being dropped by parachute and about the size of a 50 gallon oil drum . . . they contained a delayed action fuse and caused a tremendous lot of damage in built-up areas . . . they were sometimes found in the woods during daylight, suspended in the trees by the parachutes, and the fuses had to be removed by the bomb disposal units, as it was contact with the ground or hard surfaces that set the time fuse in motion.

The estate carried on, making the best of the lack of men and helped by the Land Army girls, one of whom remained at Cowdray Park as Mrs William Woodcock after the war. Every available piece of ground was cultivated, again a difficulty with the limited labour force; but older inhabitants remember that morale was extremely high in the district.

The summer of 1940, instead of seeing chukkas on the House Ground, brought the evacuation of Dunkirk, where Lord Cowdray was severely wounded. The war was to claim the lives of two of his brothers-in-law: the Hon Robin Gurdon, husband of Yoskyl Pearson, in 1942; and Lt Col George Murray, husband of Angela, in Italy in 1945. Despite losing his left arm, Lord Cowdray continued to play his part in the war as commander of the local Home Guard; and later, when polo was resumed at Cowdray, he was to play up to medium goal (and, then, to umpire) with the help of an artificial arm.

His 'contraption' was made with the help of the Roehampton Limb-Fitting Centre and his gunmakers, Purdey, enabling him to ride on the kerb with a short rein.

An integral part of the contraption was a spring for which, by trial and error, we found the correct deadweight to be 75lb, which sounds rather a lot. But it worked: I remember a fall on the River Ground, when my pony rolled right over me. I got up, thinking that I must be dead, to find my saddle bar broken but not a scratch or a bruise on me . . . I remounted and played on.

An error in the manufacture of the false arm could have resulted in serious injury. Yet nothing was going to stop John Cowdray from playing polo once the war was over, although when peace came again in 1945 the future of the game was far bleaker that it had been at the end of the Great War. Hurlingham had leased its polo grounds as allotments at the beginning of the war, and these were shortly to be purchased compulsorily by the London County Council for use as public recreation grounds. Ranelagh was in a similar situation, and while Roehampton retained one ground until 1955, polo in London was finished. The days of ten thousand polo ponies stabled in Greater London were well and truly consigned to history; and the mechanisation of the Cavalry regiments suggested that there would also be a shortage of experienced players, if indeed the game had a future.

Two country clubs - Cheshire, founded by the Cholmondeley family in 1872, and Cirencester, formed by the 7th Earl Bathurst in 1894 - were revived in 1951 and 1952 respectively. Arthur Lucas, who was to become a legendary figure in polo, started Woolmers Park in Hertfordshire, soon after the war. At Cowdray Park, the summer of 1947 saw Lord Cowdray organising three-a-side teams, initially for practice matches. On 2nd August, 1947, the *Southern Weekly News* reported the revival:

For the first time since the war, polo is being played at Cowdray Park. Teams competing in the American tournament there are Cowdray, Henley, Friar Park and Cotswold. On Tuesday night an exciting match between Cowdray and Friar Park resulted in a narrow win for the latter by 6 goals to 5.

On Wednesday evening Cotswold had Henley as their opponents, to whom they had to give a start of 3½ goals, and they soon wiped out his handicap and won by 8 goals to 3½. Cowdray, Friar Park and Cotswold each won two matches and lost one, but Cowdray were the winners in the tournament by reason of having fewer goals scored against them . . .

Peter Cruden, polo manager at Cowdray Park from 1977 to 1990, remembers coming to watch polo there while home on leave at about the same time.

COWDRAY POLO TOURNAMENT

MIDHURST.

GOODWOOD WEEK, 1947

July 29th to August 2nd.

Committee:

VISCOUNT COWDRAY.

COLONEL S. V. KENNEDY.

JOHN LAKIN, ESQ.

Special Conditions:

The game of Polo is usually played four-a-side on a ground 300 yards long by 160 yards wide. In this Tournament the teams consist of three players each and the ground is 200 yards long by 130 yards wide.

Above left: The first pre-war Cowdray Park programme, 29th July - 2nd August, 1947.

Above right: Col Sydney Kennedy, post-war umpire.

Below: John Lakin, Lord Cowdray, Daphne Lakin, Peter Dollar, 1947.

John Cowdray had ten or twelve ponies still alive after the war and brought in Harold Freeborn as his Master of Horse about 1950. In those days it was pretty nearly a women's side at Cowdray, with Yoskyl and her sisters playing. Of course, at the time I thought I could do better, having played in India!

Stuart Angell, too, recalled those immediate post-war days, with normality returning gradually to the estate:

The Cowdray Hunt again got into operation, a small pack having been retained under great difficulties and needing quite a number of hounds to make up a full pack. Hunters were not readily available and those that were needed almost breaking in again, having been turned out for a very long time. This is where Mr Harold Freeborn arrived in the picture. He began the task of taming these large animals, making them fit for Lord Cowdray and his fellow members of the hunt to ride. Mr Woodcock was back in the stables . . . polo began to be spoken of once more, a formidable task to surmount. It was at this time that lady grooms were first initiated into the stables, men being very scarce. They seemed to take to their jobs like ducks to water . . . There was also a great shortage of players and polo started with a three a side, Lord Cowdray and his sisters taking part once more, much to everyone's satisfaction and delight. Of course, the preparation of the polo grounds had to be accomplished . . . this was handed to Mr Cameron, the head gardener, and to get the River and House grounds back into shape required a great deal of effort, accomplished by horse rollers and three Dennis motor mowers, one from the house grounds, one from the golf course and the other from the woods department.

Daphne Lakin, once bored with 'girls only' polo, now played regularly for Cowdray Park with her husband, John, and her sister and brother-in-law, Yoskyl and Alistair Gibb. In those days the Lakins lived in Warwickshire - he was joint Master of the Warwickshire Hunt for many years - and would come down to Cowdray every weekend, borrowing Lord Cowdray's ponies.

It was a case of Lakins 1 and 3 and Gibbs 2 and Back at the Henley polo tournaments in 1947. I remember that we met the Jaipur side in 1948. I played to 1 in those days - they wanted to put my handicap up to 2, but I resisted: I knew that nobody would want me in their team!

For Goodwood Weekly in July, 1948, there were seven teams competing for the Cowdray Park Challenge Cup, the home team made up of 1. Major C. Davenport (1), 2. Hon Mrs J. Lakin (1), 3. Lord Cowdray (3), Bk. Lt Col J. Lakin (8). Among the spectators were Argentinian players Jack Nelson and Luis Lacey; and so impressed were they by the standard achieved at Cowdray Park, in many ways from scratch, that they invited Lord Cowdray to make up a team to compete in Buenos Aires the following year.

The visit, marking a major step in the British recovery, caused a good deal of surprise, many people considering it impossible for the English to put in a team that could compete with the other countries involved. It was clear that the team, put together under the non-playing captaincy of John Cowdray, had a difficult task ahead, and it was decided to keep the handicap of the players at 6, making an aggregate of 24. Those chosen were

Basket seats for spectators on the Lawns, 1950

Robert Skene, who had played at No. 1 in the Westchester tournament and now returned from his job in Malaya to take part; John Lakin, at No. 2, Eric Tyrrell-Martin at No. 3 and Humphrey Guinness at Back. At the time, Col Guinness was to comment:

It is a matter of great regret that at the present time there are no young players good enough to be included in the team, and this is a matter

which will, we hope, be remedied in the near future. I only hope that in spite of the fact that we are all veterans, and we will not have our own ponies with us, we will be able to hold our own. . .

It makes interesting reading to compare the handicaps of the team, a Cowdray one representing England, with their pre-war rating. When playing first-class polo regularly, Tyrrell-Martin, Lakin and Skene were handicapped at 8, Guinness at 9. But as Guinness himself remarked,

now it must be remembered that none of us have played first-class polo for 10 years and we are going out to be mounted on strange ponies on which we will play against the world's finest players in the most formidable polo country of today.

As it happened, Tyrrell-Martin, who had been in constant practice as an official of BAOC in Cairo, broke an ankle on the day he was due to leave Egypt to join the team, John Traill taking his place.

The players were allowed £3 a day for the six week stay in the Argentine, a small enough sum before devaluation; but they were enthusiastic, to say the least, although Daphne Lakin, accompanying the team, found the Argentine rather different than she had imagined.

It was polo, polo, polo, but there was no way in which women were going to be allowed to play! The routine for polo wives appeared to be looking at the ponies in the morning, then pre-luncheon drinks, then lunch followed by watching polo, the pre-dinner drinks and dinner, which often didn't even begin until 10 p.m. I rebelled after two days and found a golf course, never going near polo except for the very big matches . . .

The visit was a tremendous success. England made an auspicious debut beating Chile 12-9 in the inaugural match, a victory which shook the Chileans considerably. In a game with the Argentinian Army, England was leading 7-4 up to the start of the sixth chukka, but then the umpire gave a series of penalties against the visitors which, as the correspondent for *The Field* reported, 'proved disconcerting'. Militares beat England 11-9, but as six of the Army's goals came from penalty shots it might be fair to say that England lost on penalties alone. England also lost, 10-7, to Civiles and in the concluding match of the Argentine Open, Militares defeated Chile 10-7.

Lord Cowdray suggested a medium goal return visit for 1951 and the Argentine was represented at Cowdray Park that year for the first time. The visitors, La Espanada, were beaten in three matches for the Coronation Cup by a Cowdray Park team consisting of John Lakin, Humphrey Guinness, Gerald Balding and Alec Harper, who recalls it today as a landmark in polo history.

Programme for the Argentine Open, 1949

Polo had died completely during the war and people thought that it would be impossible to start it up again under the post-war austerity conditions. Of course, immediately after the war, polo at Cowdray was largely a case of games between the family and friends, but John Cowdray was quite determined to build up a proper team, no matter how amateur some of the matches might have appeared. Fifty ponies had been brought over from the Argentine to make up for the pre-war survivors on which we had been existing. I shall always remember how we beat the 23-goal Argentine team in those three matches at Roehampton and on the River Ground. It gave them quite a shock!

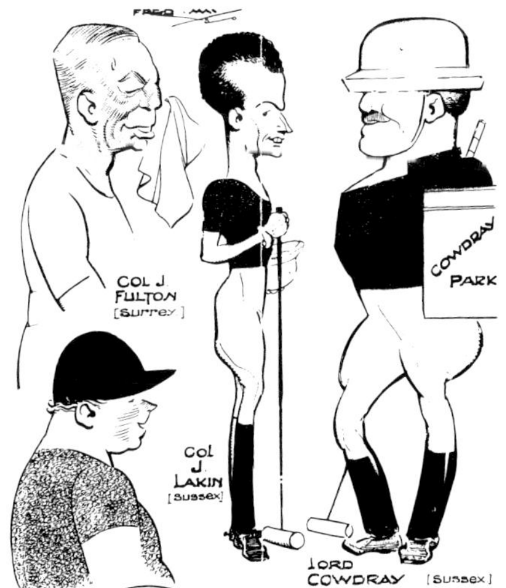

John Lakin and Lord Cowdray: Tatler's review of the 1950 Henley Polo Tournament

The England team in the USA, 1939. From left: Robert Skene, Aidan Roark, Gerald Balding, Eric Tyrrell-Martin

CHUKKA THREE

The Club Progresses

'Do it with thy might' (Cowdray family motto)

The 1950 polo season had seen the emergence of a new ground at the Duke of Sutherland's seat, Sutton Place, near Guildford. Apart from Cowdray Park, it was the only full-length, 300 yard, ground in the south of England, and the first game, on 1st July, saw a Sussex team from Cowdray Park defeat an Oxfordshire side 4-1. Lord Cowdray played at No. 2, with his twin Angela Campbell-Preston at No. 1, Col Robert Campbell-Preston at No. 3 and Alistair Gibb at Back.

In the event, the Sutton Place ground did not detract from Cowdray's renaissance and did not survive the Duke's sale of the estate. The inaugural match saw another win for Sussex in the final of the Roehampton Cup, a 5-4½ victory over Oxfordshire once again; while the end of the season, at Cowdray Park in August, was hailed by *The Times* as 'a blaze of glory', with 7,000 holidaymakers watching the final of the West Sussex Cup, to see Easebourne-based Polo Cottage beat Beechwood 9-6½ Gerald Balding, captain of the Westchester Cup team, played at No. 2 for Polo Cottage, scoring six of his team's goals including two lobbed shots from 600 yard penalties and one from within three yards of the back line from under his pony's neck.

No. 1 for Beechwood was Billy Wallace, sometime escort to Princess Margaret and for some years a familiar figure at Cowdray Park, motoring over from his home, Lavington Park (now Seaford College), near Petworth. His friendship with the Royal family supported rumours in the district that the then Princess Elizabeth and her husband were considering taking a house locally for the polo season. What became known as The Big Fib ear-marked West Dean House, near Chichester, as the house in question, and for four days in succession villagers waited expectantly in the vicinity of the entrance gates. But for some people at West Dean business boomed. 'All the housewives have been in for new hair-dos because they expected Princes Elizabeth', reported one hairdresser. 'Many of them have bought

Cup for Duke —from Princess

PRINCESS MARGARET saw the Duke of Edinburgh score the winning goal in a polo cup final at Cowdray Park yesterday—and here she is presenting the trophy to him.

Over her shoulders she draped a white cardigan. In the chill weather she watched part of the game from the car in which the Duke drove her to the polo ground. They lunched with Mr. Billy Wallace at his home.

The Queen and the Queen Mother went racing at Hurst Park—See picture on Page 7.

A cup for Prince Philip from Princess Margaret

new dresses.'

A neighbour of Lord Cowdray's to be impressed with the renaissance was Ione O'Brien, donor of the annual Park House Cup and well-loved hostess to three generations of polo players at her Park House Hotel, Bepton. She had been brought up in India, where her planter father had played, and was devoted to the game after watching her first match. Cowdray more than lived up to her accustomed standards.

I think I first saw polo at Cowdray on the House Ground in 1949. Hurlingham was finished by then and, despite the revival of other country clubs, it was Cowdray Park that became the most important in England - the home of polo. John Cowdray here, and Arthur Lucas at Woolmers Park: they were the people who got polo going again in this country, and Cowdray Park has gone from strength to strength ever since.

In my youth, of course, the Indians were the best players in the world. Nowadays, they can't produce more than a 14 goal team, so they can only play low-goal polo. But Hanut Singh and 'Jai', the Maharajah of Jaipur, used to play at Cowdray, so we had the best of both worlds, really . . .

Peter Cruden (and Katie) in the original polo office at Ambersham Cottage

Ione O'Brien's bar at Park House is lined with photographs of players and teams past and present, a veritable gallery of Cowdray Park polo. The Gracidas, Hanut Singh, Jaipur and the Hipwoods line up with 'characters' such as the comedian Jimmy Edwards, who is recalled fondly at Cowdray Park if only for his erratic playing and the 'species of carthorse' on which he thundered up the ground for his Whacko! team. Although it was before the days of the universal helicopter, several players, Edwards among them, would fly in to Ambersham, where the only memento of the Fleet Air Arm and fire-watching days were the two

Walrus hangars and the wind-sock*.

Peter Cruden, the future polo manager, was keen to play at Cowdray, having learned the game during his time as a planter in India before the war.

Ione O'Brien (left), the much loved 'first lady' of polo at Cowdray, and friend

Alec Harper had passed on some useful ponies to me up-country and I had been in touch with him since 1940, or thereabouts. When I was on leave, living in Hove, on the coast, I asked him if he thought there was any chance of my playing at Cowdray Park, and he told me to write to Lord Cowdray. Splendidly, he said 'yes' and I borrowed one of his ponies. If you were being mounted by John Cowdray, you had also to pass muster with Harold Freeborn and had to 'phone every day to see if there was a chukka free. You really waited on a call from Sydney Kennedy, the polo manager in those days. At the time, of course, I never dreamed that I would one day do his job and live in his house at Ambersham, from where the first polo office operated . . .

Having broken the ice, Peter Cruden returned to Cowdray and, in due course, was picked for a high goal side which, then, had an aggregate handicap of 17, three lower than the maximum allowed at Cowdray in 1927.

I played to 1 in those days: Rao Rajah Hanut Singh picked me out to play. He used to bring his own ponies and stable them on the River Ground.

Hanut Singh is still remembered with affection at Cowdray Park. Born in 1900, he first played for the Jodhpur Lancers when barely in his 'teens and as the writer J.N.P. Watson has noted succinctly, 'no poloist exemplified at once the unselfish sportsmanship or the high standard of polo that was typical of that era'. Hanut Singh was to be associated with

*Older residents also remember trains on the single-line track, running on the embankment behind the Ambersham grounds, waiting for as long as an hour while passengers enjoyed a match.

Jimmy Edwards with his Whacko! team, Goodwood Week, 1964

Cowdray Park for many years and, together with patrons such as Mike Holden White, the American whose Polo Cottage team was based at Easebourne, provided invaluable support for Lord Cowdray in those years of revival. Alec Harper, who was to become an international player and, later, honorary secretary of the HPA, remembers Hanut basing his assessment of players on three points:

Rao Rajah Hanut Singh, the finest polo player of his day

> *He used to say that there were men who enjoyed the game, men who played to shake up their livers and men who played for social reasons. Only the first counted to Hanut . . .*

Among the best spotted at Cowdray Park and coached by Hanut in the '50s was young Sinclair Hill, the Australian who went on to acquire a handicap of 10 and to play for the home team.

One contemporary player at Cowdray Park, Oliver Ellis, has particular reason to be grateful to Sinclair Hill. A former Cowdray Pony Club member who played his first tournament with Jersey Lilies in 1970, Oliver still recalls 'what a revelation it was' to play in medium goal matches with the Australian for two seasons.

I remember once when I lost my temper on the field: somebody from the other side had annoyed me, and with good reason. Sinclair wrote me a letter telling me not to let it get me down.

Oliver still treasures the letter, which is surely one of the best that could be sent by a seasoned player to someone still making his way in the game:

Dear Oliver,

I want to say how much I enjoyed playing with you the other day and how a very promising player you are. I think you are the best young English prospect. Keep it up.

Don't be deterred by older, less responsible people who can't behave. Keep your chin up and keep going. You're a top young man and they are fortunate to have you on the ground with them.

I am looking forward to seeing you play again.

Sinclair.

As we shall discover in due course, Sinclair Hill was not far out in his estimation of the young Oliver in 1976. Today, at the age of thirty-five, he is very much a star of the Cowdray scene.

By 1953 Cowdray Park was well on the way to becoming synonymous with polo in England, despite prognostications in the immediate post-war years that Rugby, a club that failed to survive, would take over the role of Hurlingham. Even so, not everyone was optimistic about the future of the game, thinking perhaps that a surge of enthusiasm after six years of war would shortly fade. Writing in *The Field* of 12th August, 1954, Brigadier Jack Gannon, a formidable player in his day and remembered now in the Jack Gannon Trophy at Cowdray Park, noted:

A gloomy chap remarked to me last year that, in three years, polo in England would pass away, as there were not enough young players to replace the old 'uns as they fell out. I am not laying off my gentle bet to the contrary, for in Goodwood Week at Cowdray Park (this year) the Holden White Cup for low-goal teams had 17 entries, and looking through the list I make out that 38 of the players never had a stick in their hands before the war.

Gannon's optimism was not misplaced. Indeed, the previous year Cowdray Park had been the setting for the Coronation Cup with teams competing from the USA, the Argentine, Brazil, Chile and Spain; and over a thousand cars and coaches brought an estimated 15,000 spectators to see the Argentine beat England in the final. Admittedly, the final of the British Open Championship for the Gold Cup, the red-letter day in polo, in 1990 attracted around six thousand spectators; but 1953 was, after all, a year of national celebration.

This was one of the greatest polo seasons at Cowdray (recalled Stuart Angell, who helped to prepare the grounds) and the public certainly saw what real polo was like and gained an appetite for more. I had to go to the London Docks to help with the luggage, in which case a Bedford van was used, or drive one of the horse boxes. This was a great experience for me, to see the ponies standing in their little cubicles on the deck of the Blue Star Line boats. The journey usually took at least three weeks from South America: if the sea was very rough, the waves would wash right over the deck and over the ponies' legs. The grooms liked this, as they said the sea water strengthened the legs. Each pony was inspected by a vet before it was allowed off the boat, then put into a proper one-horse container and lifted by crane clear of the boat, put down on the dockside, taken out of the container and gently walked up and down before being put into the horse box, to get the circulation moving.

Inevitably, there were delays, particularly when grooms speaking no English disembarked. Customs officials, too, could prove recalcitrant and Stuart Angell remembered an incident when a New Zealand team came over for the first time.

I got as far as the dock gates on my way out and was sent back to the sheds, made to unload, and had to go up again the next day. This was because we had ten bales of New Zealand hay on board the van, and we had no clearance for the hay. The two players who were with me spent two or three hours trying to get it cleared, but failed to do so. Our custom people were most unpopular, but I suppose it was right, as the hay could have been infected . . .

The Coronation Cup tournament removed any lingering doubts about the future of English polo. First presented in 1911, to mark the coronation of George V, it was until 1939 played for by the winners of the London Open tournaments, Hurlingham, Roehampton, Ranelagh and the Inter-Regimental. Alec Harper, who played No. 1 in the England team with Gerald Balding at 2, Humphrey Guinness at 3 and John Lakin at Back, remembers that the tournament came to Cowdray Park on Lord Cowdray's initiative. In the final, England was beaten 8-7 by the Argentine team of Mihanovich, Lalor, Alberdi and Braun: an honourable defeat and Cowdray Park, which had supplied the England team, could bask in the reflected glory of the occasion.

The burst of popularity in Coronation Year encouraged the club to consider bringing polo 'within the pocket of the £10 a week man', according

The Queen and Prince Philip join Lord and Lady Cowdray for the Coronation Cup final, 1953

to the *Brighton Evening Argus,* which noted that players could hire a pony from the Cowdray stables and play one chukka for £1. At the same time, a spokesman for the club stressed the importance of encouraging young ex-Servicemen who took up polo in the Forces to train for places on the tournament teams. The only way was to provide them with free ponies and facilities to play regularly, otherwise polo would be beyond their pocket.

So we are encouraging the masses to come and pay to see polo played at our club. We want to see polo recognised as one of our popular national sporting events and to draw a regular weekend crowd of 5,000 or 6,000 to Cowdray Park.

Everything possible was done to encourage new spectators, perhaps some of them potential players. Motor coaches were admitted to the edge of the grounds, so that passengers, in the quaint phraseology of the *Brighton Evening Argus,* 'can either view the game from their seats or sprawl on the grass and watch'. Pedestrians paid 1s to watch Saturday matches and, certainly, Lord Cowdray was the first English polo patron to act on the possibility of attracting the public at large, interesting them with a programme showing the names of the players, their ponies and other relevant information. Commentators, too, were introduced and while elderly players, expert in their day, tended to grumble at perpetual explanations of the game, they recognised the value of a commentary in helping to fill the ground. Alec Harper was sometimes told off to do the commentary:

There was not really an official commentator then; no-one like Terry Hanlon or Peter Holman, who we have today. John Moran, who had played polo as a planter in India, and I would do it from time to time, or perhaps a local player who knew everyone would take over . . .

The crowds continued to flock to Cowdray for polo which, in the '50s, consisted of weekend matches, the week being devoted to chukkas. 'Perhaps a national love of the horse is still ingrained in the English make-up, in spite of the mechanical trend of modern life,' mused Jack Gannon, searching for an explanation for the 'remarkable numbers of the public' who turned up.

Few of them are likely to have played polo, or to have had anything to do with it. Possibly, they may have started to come to polo as a reason for the weekend drive; yet I feel sure that many who originally came for the drive now contrive to watch the galloping game for its own sake.

Stuart Angell was one of four gatemen during the 1953 season, and noted the very large crowds watching both matches and chukkas at weekends.

Cup presented by Her Majesty Queen Elizabeth.

FINAL THE CORONATION CUP

ARGENTINA V ENGLAND

Colours (Light Blue & White Stripe) — Colours (Blue)

(6 Chukkers)

No.	Player	Handicap
1	E. BRAUN - MENENDEZ''	3
2	E. LALOR''	6
3	A. MIHANOVICH'	4
Back	J. C. ALBERDI''	9
	Handicap Total	22

No.	Player	Handicap
1	Lt. COL. A. F. HARPER'	5
2	CAPT. G. BALDING'	6
3	Lt. COL. H. P. GUINNESS'	6
Back	JOHN LAKIN'''	6
	Handicap Total	23

E. Lalor injured in 2nd Chukker, but resumed after 5 minutes

Chukka	Recd.	Goals
1	I	1
2		—
3	I	1
4	III	3
5	I	1
6	I	1
	Total	7

Chukka	Recd.	Goals
1	I	1
2		—
3		—
4		—
5	II	2
6	III	3
	Total	6

Date Sunday, 21st June 1953 — Ground Lawns

The public side of the ground was often four deep in cars, and this encouraged the public to come very early and get a front parking place . . . I was one of the gatemen for about twelve years and in the early days one of us had to be on duty at 11 a.m. to deal with the early arrivals, who usually picnicked if the weather was suitable, as the games did not start until 3.15 p.m.

The Queen and Prince Philip in the pony lines, 1954

The questions we had to answer were nobody's business, as 80 per cent of the public who came in by car had never seen a game of polo, or had any idea of the game. Those that had asked if the centre positions were full and were told that cars started coming in at 11 a.m. seemed flabbergasted; but we often noticed that these were the first in the next weekend and drove to the grounds like demons. You would also get the person who did not want to go to polo at all, but had followed the rest of the cars. When you went to collect their money, which was 10s per car, they decided not to come in. The Works Yard gate was the worst one for this kind of thing happening, as there was not a lot of room for cars to turn . . .

One of the best gates for the number of cars remembered by Mr Angell was on a Whit Monday on the Ambersham grounds, now devoted to polo and helping to relieve the strain on the three original grounds. It was the first time a motor race meeting had been held at nearby Goodwood on this particular holiday; the car parks at the circuit were soon full and disappointed spectators came on to polo instead.

No. 1 and 2 ground were end to end running from north to south. I was on the middle gate, there was a stiff breeze blowing and I had to keep pressing the notes - it was still 10s per car - down into my haversack. I don't think I took my eyes off my books of tickets for what seemed like hours and, when we checked up, I had taken over 700.

Even those who had not set out with the intention of watching polo were apt to become addicted to the fastest game in the world. One Sunday in the '50s a family - parents and four young children - turned up at Ambersham in a far from holiday mood. They had been driving to the seaside, the weather had changed to rain and polo was suggested by the wife as an alternative to a wet afternoon on the beach. Stuart Angell was again on the gate.

They argued a great deal and the husband was quite rude to me. However, they paid and came in and parked. The sun was out and there were three very good games. The following Sunday they came in again . . . the parents walked over to me and apologised for being short-tempered the previous weekend. 'In fact you did me a jolly good turn.' said the husband. 'My entrance fee was a very cheap day out, we were all thrilled with the polo, the children were able to run around and go and watch the ponies and we stayed and had a picnic tea, as well as lunch. From now on its polo on Sundays for us. If I had gone to the coast it would have cost me three times the amount, for rides in the fun fair for the children - and they have been worrying all the week for Sunday to come so they can go and see those lovely ponies again . . .

Score books at Cowdray Park start with a semi-final of the Tyro Cup, played at Ambersham on Saturday, 9th May, 1953, a warm and sunny day on which the home team won a four chukka game 6-4.

Cowdray Park *(Orange)*	Polo Cottage *(Maroon and Canary)*
1. Lt Col W.H.G. Gerrard-Leigh (1)	1. F.L. Withers (2)
2. Lt Col A.F. Harper (5)	2. Brig the Hon R.G. Hamilton-Russell (3)
3. Lt Col P.W. Dollar (4)	3. Col G.H. Critchley (4)
Bk. HRH The Duke of Edinburgh (2)	Bk. W. Holden White (3)

In the final, eight days later, Cowdray Park lost 2-6 to Beechwood.

Joe Plotka, in exile from his native Poland after the war, came to work on the Cowdray Estate in 1946. A familiar figure at Cowdray Park and Ambersham during the season, as gateman to the members' enclosure (and the scourge of potential gate-crashers), he also recalls the early crowds.

I remember one afternoon in particular on the River Ground. I was still working on the farm then and had been home to change and went down to the River Ground to find my wife, who used to take our tea with her. Usually, I could spot her from a distance because our dog would be beside her. This time, however, there was just a sea of people and I had to squeeze my way between hundreds of pairs of legs . . .

Cowdray Park, winners of the Tyro Cup, 13th May, 1956. They beat Hanut Singh's Ratanada $7^1/_2$-3. From left: Lord Cowdray, Daphne Lakin, Sharman Douglas (who presented the cup), John Lakin and Peter Dollar

Sadly, there is no record of attendance at that first recorded game at Ambersham which was followed by a four chukka match between Beechwood and The Pirates, the green-shirted Beechwood beating their red-clad opponents 6-$4^1/_2$. But an additional attraction to the public in those post-war years was Prince Philip, a classic example of the young players whom the polo manager, Lt Col Philip 'Bolshie' Tatham, appointed in 1953 after a career in the Indian Army, hoped to draw to Cowdray Park.

Taught by his uncle, Lord Mountbatten*, while serving with the Navy in Malta, the prince's handicap had just been raised from 2 to 3 when he played for Cowdray Park in the final of the high handicap Smith Ryland Cup on 20th June, 1954, on Ambersham No. 1 ground.

Cowdray Park *(Orange)*	The Greyhounds *(Red)*
1. HRH The Duke of Edinburgh (3)	1. Major J.P. Robinson (3)
2. Lt Col P.W. Dollar (4)	2. C. Smith Ryland (3)
3. Rao Rajah Hanut Singh (5)	3. Lt Col A.F. Harper (4)
Bk. J. Lakin (6)	Bk. Col G.H. Critchley (4)

*Before the war, Lord Mountbatten had run the Adsdean team, based not far from Cowdray Park at Lavant. The latest Mountbatten to play at Cowdray is the 4th Marquess of Milford Haven (2), born in 1961.

Prince Philip's Mariners team, 1954. Alec Harper, 'an honorary sailor', is second from right. From left are Robert de Pass, Prince Philip and Philip Maunder

The cup had been presented by Charles Smith Ryland, who played originally in Mike Holden White's Polo Cottage team (and, later, for Cowdray Park) and who, two years previously, had married Lord Cowdray's neice, Jeryl Gurdon, daughter of Yoskyl. Prince Philip scored two goals and the home team beat Greyhounds 5-2½. Later the same day, he was in third position in a Sea Horses 'B' team, beating Cowdray Park in a league match 5-3.

A *Sunday Pictorial* journalist, Rex North, suggested to Lord Cowdray that 'it looks as if you use the Duke of Edinburgh too much for publicity purposes'; to which blatantly unfair charge Lord Cowdray replied: 'It is difficult to stop publicity on the Duke.' In any case, it was hardly the club's fault. An announcement, purporting to come from the publicity agents of Roehampton Club, appeared in the Press informing polo- (or Royal-) watchers that if they telephoned WELbeck 3776 before a polo playing weekend, they would discover if the Prince was to be at Cowdray that weekend.

Susan Maxwell recalls the enterprise of a local blacksmith:

He had a pile of horseshoes outside the forge, which he said had been worn by Prince Philip's ponies. He sold them to the locals and made quite a packet!

Alec Harper, a soldier, became an honorary sailor for a time in the same season:

Prince Philip had formed a 12-goal Naval team with Philip Maunder, Robert de Pass, who had been Mountbatten's flag lieutenant in Malta, and (Major-General) Sir Robert Neville, who had just retired as Governor of the Bahamas. Neville, who was getting on for 60 at the time, broke his collarbone playing chukkas, and I was drafted in by the Mariners team to take his place. I remember that we all wore white sailors' shirts - and we won everything in that first year.

So intense was public interest by now that Cowdray Park achieved mention on the air. For example, *Radio Times* of 23rd July, 1954, included in its programme for Saturday, 31st July, a twenty-minute commentary from Cdr J.G. Aitchison and Henry Riddell on the second half of the Cowdray Park Challenge Cup final. It was sandwiched between two extremely popular regular items: *Saturday Matinee* and a repeat of Jack Buchanan's *Home and Away*.

Alec Harper's honorary position in the Senior Service lasted until

Major Archie David (right) was playing polo until well into his 70s

Prince Philip with Archie David's financial help and Lord Cowdray's expert advice, formed the Household Brigade Club (now the Guards) on Smith's Lawn, Windsor Great Park, in 1955.

Major Archie David was a familiar figure at Cowdray for many years. A tea planter in the Far East, he returned to his home, Friar Park, near Henley-on-Thames*, in the 1930s and started the Friar Park polo team. After the war he did much to revive polo in England and played on his own grounds - like Ambersham they had served as an airfield - until the formation of the Household Brigade Club.

He was very secretive about his age (recalls Lord Patrick Beresford) but I can remember him playing in the final of the Harrison Cup at Cowdray in 1964 and he must have been 75 at the time.

David had inaugurated the Friar Park Cup soon after starting his team; when he died, in 1972, the Guards Club renamed it the Archie David Cup as an appropriate memorial. Today, it claims to be the low-goal tournament attracting the highest entry, perhaps because it comes mid-season. The Ambersham grounds are the setting for a number of qualifiers and semi-finals.

The 1955 season at Cowdray Park was overshadowed by tragedy, when Lt Col Alistair Gibb, who had married the widowed Yoskyl Pearson, was killed during the semi-final of the Subsidiary Cup on 29th July. The four chukka match, between Cotswold Park, for which Gibb played No. 1, and Woolmers Park, was 5-2 in favour of Cotswold Park on a fine summer evening and three and a half minutes of the final chukka had been played when the accident occured. The match was abandoned.

Yet, tragedy apart, there was no doubt that Lord Cowdray's vision of the estate as the home of English polo, and as host to international players, had been achieved in a few brief years. Matches were still played at weekends, or every evening during Goodwood Week, and the extra ground at Ambersham guaranteed that polo was possible whatever the weather.

While several officers of the 10th Hussars - the regiment that had played in the inaugural match at Hounslow nearly a century earlier - took up polo, hopes of a major revival in regimental polo proved forlorn. At the start of the 1954 season, a 10th Hussars team was beaten by Cowdray Park,

*Friar Park is now owned by George Harrison, the musician and former Beatle, Archie David's grounds were retained by Guards in case of an emergency but have never been used.

Lord Cowdray in 1955

10-4, in a qualifying match for the Tyro Cup, once a regular feature of the London season at Hurlingham and first presented by Major C.W. Peters in 1920. Semi-finals for this medium-goal trophy continue to open the season at Cowdray Park today, but regimental polo has never again been a serious force.

Regimental polo is fairly low goal (notes Alec Harper) and there is not a single regimental team which can add up to two figures nowadays. It just doesn't hold up to anything at Cowdray Park.

Local teams were formed, including Fernhurst, the patron of which was Jack Robinson, a predecessor of Alec Harper at Ambersham Farm and the uncle of Sarah Sugden, well-known today as the energetic assistant polo manager at Cowdray. Sarah Sugden remembers hacking over to Ambersham from Henley, north of Midhurst, to watch polo in her childhood.

Really dedicated people became members of the club and were at Cowdray every weekend to follow the game. They soon realised what good value they were getting for their subscription - where else could one see*

*It remains good value at £50 for its 700 non-playing members and £1,000 for the current 100 playing members, the lowest fees of the four principal clubs and the only one not to charge players entrance fees. There are now 10 grounds at Cowdray. Of the other 'big' clubs, Cirencester has six, Guards five and the Royal Berkshire three.

so many days of polo? Nowadays, the casual visitor might think that attendance at a low- or medium-goal match is not particularly high, but the spectators are all members of the club, which is the point to remember.

Another familiar figure at Cowdray Park, who saw the club grow in popularity, is Brian Bethell, who took over as Lord Cowdray's Master of the Horse from Harold Freeborn twenty years ago and retired in 1985. A Gloucestershire man, he played for Cirencester before moving to Cowdray Park and would come down for matches in Goodwood Week in the '50s.

I remember Hanut Singh saying that he preferred to play at Cowdray Park because one saw much better polo than was possible in India, and he was not alone in holding that opinion. I suppose that competitions were different in the 1950s; there were not so many teams taking part as there are today, but even then Cowdray was rather special to players because of the good level of polo. Of course, people wanted to win, but that was never an overriding factor here: it was the game that counted.

Annette Bethell, Brian's wife, has for the last decade organised chukkas at Cowdray Park, as well as coping with the problems of finding accommodation for overseas players.

Sarah Sugden

Brian and Annette Bethell

In the early days, when we came here on holiday and when Brian was playing here in the Cirencester team, Lord Cowdray was mounting many of the players. There was, even then, a tremendous emphasis on encouraging young players, although the inexperienced would not be given a stick when they went into their first chukka. They had to learn to ride in a match first. 'Bolshie' Tatham would grant permission to play only if one was proficient.

Brian Bethell stopped playing polo two years ago, although he is still an honorary playing member at Cowdray Park. However, his son, Chris, who has a current handicap of 4, is among the leading thirty-four English players from seven clubs- no less than half of them coming from Cowdray Park. His mother also recalls the social side of Goodwood Week at Cowdray in that momentous decade after the war.

There was a party every night. People like Eric Moller, patron of the Jersey Lilies team, threw enormous parties and everyone stayed on for them after a match. There was no rushing off by helicopter in those days!

Mollie Tatham, widow of Lt Col 'Bolshie' Tatham, polo manager at Cowdray Park for twenty-three seasons - from April, 1953, to August, 1976 - recalls 'the most wonderful parties':

There would be drink galore and a beautiful sit-down dinner, with dancing or Bridge afterwards. The Cowdrays always gave a lovely party with their gardens illuminated. Then there were many barbecues, usually with awful half-cooked meat: I loathed them! I used to say to Bolshie: 'Need we go, must we go?' His reply was that he had to get his umpires. 'If you ask them in the office they say 'No'; but if you ask them at a party, they always say 'Yes'. So the polo book went with him. I had to collect all my uncooked meat in a bag in my handbag and take it home to the dogs - I could hardly chuck it over the wall. The dogs were very happy . . .

Col Tatham insisted on punctuality in matches, starting a 'not very good game' at 2 pm, the best matches, then as now, at 3 pm.

The whistle went and the game started, even if a patron had not arrived. Anyone who was late had late chukkas for the rest of the season. This made a good deal of trouble to begin with, but soon everyone got the message and many said they preferred it.

Bolshie was sometimes made to umpire - he loathed it and said he didn't know how to do it! In India, where he had been in the Cavalry before

No polo today! The flooding Rother stops play on the River Ground

the awful days of mechanisation, the few people who liked umpiring had to pass a test, and then there was an official umpires list. Bolshie tried to bring this in at Cowdray but failed.

There was one player who always gave his false teeth to the umpire to hold! Bolshie did not much care for this and handed the teeth to me. I didn't care for it either and as no one else would have them I put them in the car - and then forgot whereabouts. It was such a frequent occurrence that I bought a box for them, and they had their own place in the car after that!

Undoubtedly, one of the attractions of Cowdray was (and remains) the fact that rain rarely stopped play. The River Ground drains quickly into the Rother and the House Ground has a pronounced slope, again beneficial. Brenda Freeling, who came as a groom to Cowdray in 1955, initially for six months but remained on the estate, remembers that play was always possible on the House Ground. It is interesting that at the start of the 1991 season, an inch of rain at Ambersham in early May prompted a move to the House Ground, reserved usually for chukkas, for an afternoon of medium-goal Texaco Trophy league matches. A month later,

Col 'Bolshie' Tatham and his wife, Mollie, enjoy a break from polo

the final of the low-goal Barrett Cup, and its subsidiary, were also played on the House Ground; although at the same time there was some irritation among spectators that the final of the high-goal Cooch Behar Cup was postponed at the last minute until the following weekend. 'Rain never stops play' was the general comment!

When Brenda Freeling arrived, chukkas were played on the House Ground on Wednesdays at 3 pm and on Fridays at 4.30 pm. Ponies began to arrive at the Cowdray stables towards the end of January.

We had three distinct stables in those days: Cowdray House took twenty ponies, Todham twenty-one. These were for the 'A' club players. The Priory stables were reserved for the 'B' club - younger players and those with a low handicap.

The grooms were each allocated a player - I mounted Col Gerald Critchley every season - so that we would get to know them, and they us.

Pony lines at Cowdray Park, 1950s

Gerald Critchley had the Greyhounds team, which included Col Harper and Col Tatham. When the age of an average team in those days was totted up it was quite impressive!

When Roehampton closed its sole surviving ground in 1955 - Alec Harper says that it could no longer attract the London public - there was an hiatus about where the principal cup of the season should find a new home. Indeed, what was to be the principal cup? From 1876 to 1939 Hurlingham had hosted matches for the Champion Cup, but that had failed to survive the war. With Roehampton no longer functioning, eyes may have turned towards Ham Polo Club, founded in 1931 with one full-sized ground on the still largely rural Ham Common. After the war, however, Ham also lost its home ground and while matches were played from 1947 in Richmond Park, through the courtesy of the Royal Bailiff, the turn of the country club, not the suburban, had come.

Smith's Lawn, and Prince Philip's new club, took over as the tournament ground for the Coronation Cup; but with or without royal participation, Cowdray Park was drawing both players and public.

It is interesting to contrast Stuart Angell's memories with the remarks of American polo writer Peter Vischer in *Horse & Horseman* concerning the 'attitude towards the public' of English polo clubs in 1935.

They want the public's money at the gate at Hurlingham, provided it is the kind of public that can pay $5 to $25 for a seat. But they do not want the public at all at Ranelagh or Roehampton, because they have no facilities for keeping them out of the clubhouse . . . Yet they 'encourage' the public to come by giving each member vouchers that will admit his friends, usually at 3 shillings each. Ladies get in free, which accounts for the fact that at an ordinary club match in London half of the spectators are dear old ladies over the age of 60. Nobody could possibly get interested in polo in London by going to a match as he might go to a tennis match or other sporting event. Those in control of polo activities in London make it entirely too difficult for a sport enthusiast to become even a casual spectator.

Vischer felt that the organisation of polo in England - at least in town - was too loosely knit and lacked the support of the various factors that made the game possible in its best form: patrons, players, club officials and staff, the Press and public. The game, he alleged, was still largely in the control of the military and not in the hands of polo players themselves.

A year later, *The Field* complained that 'English polo seems to be absurdly chained to the chariot wheels of a London social season, which itself revolves around the axis of the debutante, and every reasonable step

Enjoying polo at Cowdray Park

should be taken to provide players with every possible chukker'; while *The Times* commented, after the first match for the Ranelagh Cup, 'that when the best entertainment in London was offered, so few people were there to see it.'

Twenty years later, however, all was changed. In 1956 Cowdray Park was the leading English club, and that year was to see the inauguration of what soon became the leading tournament: the British Open Championship for the Cowdray Park Gold Cup. The successor to the Champion Cup, it was to place Cowdray Park well and truly on the international polo map.

An impression of Hanut Singh before the war

CHUKKA FOUR

The Gold Cup

'How long does it take to get a goal?' the Maltese Cat answered. 'For pity's sake, don't run away with the notion that the game is half-won just because we happen to be in luck now. They'll run you into the grand-stand if they can . . . ' (Kipling, 'The Maltese Cat', from *The Day's Work*, 1898)

The Gods who preside over polo decided that 1956 would be remembered not only as the inaugural year of the Cowdray Park Gold Cup but for the wettest polo season since before the war. It rained at Cowdray Park throughout June yet, with the exception of the Cowdray Park Challenge Cup, initiated in 1948, the major tournaments - for the Gold Cup, the Harrison Cup and the Holden White Cup - were concluded despite appalling conditions.

Writing the introduction to the following year's Hurlingham Polo Association handbook, Lord Cowdray, then chairman of the association, could look back with satisfaction on the first Gold Cup season.

The season was distinguished by the arrival of two visiting teams to play with us. A New Zealand, Aotea, team bringing their own ponies, captained by Hamish Wilson, and the Argentine 20-goal Los Indios, captained by Senor A. Heguy . . . The New Zealand ponies, which arrived rather late in the season, took time to acclimatise. Aotea won the Neil Haig Cup at Roehampton and their sportsmanship in coming so great a distance was much appreciated.

There was an unforeseen sequel to the New Zealand visit. Aotea, named after an early Maori canoe which, in legend, reached the shores of New Zealand six centuries ago, had an aggregate handicap of 23. Looking back on their arrival, Lord Cowdray recalls that he considered them to be grossly over-handicapped and put them down on paper to 16.

They left with an aggregate of 9. Because they had not done so very well, no-one thought very much of their ponies - they were all in snaffles, for one thing. I bought the lot for about £450, and one of them was Little

FINAL — THE COWDRAY PARK GOLD CUP.

LOS INDIOS (ARGENTINE) V COWDRAY PARK

Colours White, black band — Colours Orange

HIGH HANDICAP 20–17 — 6 CHUKKERS

LOS INDIOS (ARGENTINE)

No.	Player	Handicap
1	JORGE MARIN MARENO	5
2	JOSE NAGORE	5
3	ANTONIO HEGUY	6
Back	JUAN ETCHEVERS' HARRIET	4
	Handicap Total	20

COWDRAY PARK

No.	Player	Handicap
1	LT. COL. A.F. HARPER	4
2	C. SMITH RYLAND	4
3	RAO RAJAH HANUT SINGH	6
Back	J. LAKIN	6
	Handicap Total	20

LOS INDIOS (ARGENTINE)

Chukka		Goals
	Recd.	—
1	1.	1
2	1.1.	2
3	1.	1
4	1.1.	2
5	1.	1
6	1.1.	2
	Total	9

COWDRAY PARK

Chukka		Goals
	Recd.	—
1	–	–
2	–	–
3	1.1.	2
4	–	–
5	1.	1
6	1.	1
	Total	4

Date SUNDAY. 5th AUGUST 1956

Time 3–10 P.M.

Ground LAWNS

Weather Conditions BRIGHT and SUNNY after HEAVY RAIN.

Jenny who turned out to be just the sort of pony I loved. You had only to touch the reigns and she was off; touch them again and she stopped. After I gave up playing, I umpired on her for several years . . .

A 23-goal team from the Argentine had been beaten with distinction on the River Ground in 1951 but had redeemed their national pride two years later, in the Coronation Cup final. However, despite a strong opposition and despite the weather, it seemed as though 1956 would see a British victory. The Cowdray Park team was a formidable combination of Alec Harper (5), Charles Smith Ryland (4), Hanut Singh (6) and John Lakin (6), even though Col Harper recalls that the aggregate age was around the 200 year mark. Los Indios, in white with black bands, consisted of Jorge Marin Moreno (5), Jose Nagore (5), Antonio Heguy (6) and Juan Etchevers Harriet (4).

It is worth pausing for a moment to examine the average handicap of the day through the list of playing members at Cowdray Park in 1956.

Anderson, Col W.A.	1
Anderson, Capt S.N.	1
Archer Shee, Brig J.P.	3
Bachan, Singh	0
Bagnell, Capt W.D.A.	0
Baig, Brig M.A.	5
Bengough, Capt P.H.	-2
Bennett, D.	-2
Bijai Singh, Kunwar	4
Boord, Lt Col O.L.	1
Brecknock, Lord	1
Campbell-Preston, Hon Mrs	0
Carey, Major J. de B.	-1
Cowdray, Viscount	1
Craig Harvey, A.J.	1
Critchley, Col G.H.	4
Dawnay, Major Gen D.	3
de Lisser, W.	2
de Pass, Cmdr R.E.F., RN	1
Dollar, Col P.W.	3
Farmer, Cmdr L.G.H., RN	1
Firbank, S.C.	-2
Foster, Capt J.H.	0
Freeborn, H.	3
Glanville, G.D.	-2
Hamilton Russell, Brig Hon R.G.	3
Hanut Singh, Rao Rajah	6
Hari Singh, Kunwar	3
Harper, Lt Col A.F., DSO	5
Harris, Col S.W.	1
Hedley, Capt G.	1
Hicks, R.M.	1
Hilder, Major T.	0
Hinde, Major Gen Sir R.W.	3
Hobson, Brig R. W.	4
Holden-White, M.	3
Jaipur, HH The Maharajah of	5
Jones, Capt H.L.M.	-1
Joynson, Brooke	0
Lakin, Hon Mrs J.	1
Lakin, J.	6
Ley, I.F.	-2
Little, D.F.	2
Llewellyn-Palmer, Lt Col A.	2
Maunder, Lt J.W.M., RN	1
Moller, E.B.	0
McNeill, Col J.M.	1
Neville, Major Gen Sir R.A.R.	1
Noble, Lt Col F.B.B.	1
Oram, Lt Cmdr J., RN	0

O'Reilly, Lt D.A.P., RN 0
Pitman, J.H. ....-1
Pretyman, W. 2
Ramsay, A.C. ....-2
Rayner, R. ....-2
Riley-Smith, W.H.D. 3
Riley-Smith, J. ....-2
Robinson, Major J.P. 2
St. Aubyn, Capt T.E. 0
Scott, Major J.W. ....-2
Smith, Lt Col D.F.G. 1
Smith Ryland, C.M.T. 4
Spencer, Capt R.P.M. 1
Stirum, Capt C.S. ....-2
Tatham, Lt Col P.R. 2
Troubridge, Lt E., RM ....-1
Troubridge, Lt P., RN ....-1
Turner, Lt Col C.G.N. 0
Wallace, W.E. 1
Warner Bolton, H. 1
Wilson, P.R. 3
Wilson, R.P. ....-2
Withers, F.L. 2
Withers, P.M. 0

Handicapping is always a moot point, and Tony Tame, Clerk of the Works at Cowdray Park from 1958 until his retirement in 1987, wonders if today players are handicapped too highly.

One of the highest goal players in my day was John Lakin at 6, and to my mind he was far better than any of the 10-goalers who come here now. Of course, they all seem to be well-mounted today, although many of the ponies seem mediocre compared with the days when they cost £1,000 a head!

John Lakin, a member of the ill-fated English team in the pre-war Westchester Cup tournament, had married Daphne Pearson in 1939. As early as 1938 he had received a glowing tribute in the pages of the American magazine, *Horse & Horseman*, as the international teams for the following season were announced:

John Lakin . . . a young player who has come to the front this season. He may not find a place for 1939, but he has the makings in him, and the experience of the trip must do him a lot of good. His riding has improved this year, in a polo sense, he has an eye like a hawk and may turn into a great player. One of the greatest failings in English polo is that when a young player begins to show any aptitude he is at once put in at No. 3 or back. The result is that we have a lot of fairly useful men for those positions, but are lamentably short of competent forwards. The powers that be have, at last, realised this and the intention is to develop this promising young performer in the front of the game.

At the time of his much-lamented death in 1989, Lakin was the last survivor of the 1939 England team. The American journalist was not mis-

House Ground with Cowdray House at left

House Ground

taken in his estimation of the newcomer: he played for England again in 1951 and 1953 and was perhaps the leading English player until his enforced retirement, on medical advice, in 1962.

Lord Cowdray (centre) with the 1958 Cowdray Park Gold Cup team. From left: Hanut Singh, Alec Harper, John Lakin, Peter Dollar

In 1956 his team beat Los Indios in two 20-goal tournaments but the Argentines retaliated to win the Cowdray Park Gold Cup in the final, defeating the home team 9-4. *The Times* called the result 'a full and satisfying revenge':

Cowdray had already beaten them twice . . . so the final meeting was something of an occasion. Cowdray Park had their combination broken up, and their No. 1 (Alec Harper), grand player though he is, is not a No. 1. All too often he was found mixing it in defence and generally showed a tendency to hang back. This is not surprising, for he is a No. 3 or a back by choice and practice. This was a great occasion for the visitors and they thoroughly deserved their success . . .

John Lakin was badly knocked about by a pony's head in a collision early in the game and was thereafter unable to take a nearside back-hander, perhaps his most brilliant shot. But *The Times* was not altogether fair to Alec Harper: he chalked up Cowdray's first and second goals in the third chukka, and it was his Los Indios opposite number, Marin Moreno, who played the best for the visitors. Even before the match the Argentinians had been optimistic: 5th August had seen heavy showers in the morning, although the afternoon was bright and sunny for the 3.10 pm match. Yet while the ground had dried quickly, the Lawns cut up badly, conditions which suited the short passing game of Los Indios.

Disappointment apart, the new tournament - at the time the only open tournament for teams of 20 to 15 goals - had proved an important point. In 1919 *Polo Monthly* had suggested that Cowdray Park could well become the centre for a group of southern tournaments. The Gold Cup had taken the number of tournaments played there to four, no small achievement in a lean decade.

That day, 5th August 1956, was exceptionally busy. The Gold Cup final was followed at 4.55 p.m. by the semi-final of the medium-goal Harrison Cup, a four-chukka match between the maroon-shirted Friar Park and the yellow-clad Silver Leys, who won 5-4; and at 5.50 p.m. by the semi-final for the Subsidiary Cup, with the maroon and canary shirts of Polo Cottage beating the green and grey Warren Mere 7-6. An hour later the familiar orange shirts of a low-goal Cowdray team, comprising R.N. Hutchings (-1), T. Marriage (1), Lord Cowdray (1) and Major C.H.S. Dixon (2) lost 3-0 to the red-shirted Cheshire in the semi final of the low handicap Holden White Cup.

The next day, renewed heavy rain during the morning saw all matches transferred to the House Ground, where Windsor Park, with Prince Philip as back, beat Silver Leys 6½-5 in the Harrison final; Warren Mere beat Cheshire 5-2½ in the Holden White final and Polo Cottage lost 10-12 to Hanut Singh's Ratanada in the last match for the Subsidiary Cup.

The second year of the Gold Cup, 1957, saw no less than five overseas teams visiting Cowdray Park, including a 20-goal Indian team, a 12-goal Argentine team, Media Luna, and another from Jamaica. For the Gold Cup season, Baron Elie de Rothschild brought his Casarejos from Paris, while Evelyn de Rothschild came over with Centaurs. The home team, Lt Col Peter Dollar (2), John Lakin (6), Alec Harper (4) and Gerald Critchley (3) lost 6-5, but after extra time, in the semi-finals and their opponents, Windsor Park, went on to beat Casarejo 5-3 and carry off the cup. Lord Cowdray recalled the match on 14th July:

It was a fine performance on a very wet ground, with Col Humphrey Guinness (No. 2 for Windsor Park) pulling out his pre-war class and the Duke of Edinburgh at the top of his form. Cowdray Park followed this

AOS

Wolters
HOLDERS
SLADMORE
KGG I

example by defeating Centaurs ($4\frac{1}{2}$-3) in the Cowdray Park Challenge Cup during Goodwood Week in proverbial glorious weather. They were brilliantly led by John Lakin: hard riding and close marking just won them the cup.

Cowdray Park was to win the Gold Cup for the first time on 13th July 1958, defeating Arthur Lucas's Woolmers Park 10-3, on a dull and windy afternoon on the Lawns. Peter Dollar was at No. 1, supported by Harper, Hanut Singh and Lakin; facing them where J. Marin Moreno, the former Los Indios player, whose handicap remained at 5, John Lucas (3), son of the Woolmers Park patron, P. Llorente (5) and R. Braun-Menendez (4).

The next two years saw Casarejo victorious, beating Cowdray Park 7-6 in 1959 and Centaurs 8-7 in 1960. Their second win is something of a record in Cowdray history - the first time that two Rothschild-sponsored teams had fought for the premier cup. This time the weather on 10th July was wet and windy and Jorge Marin Moreno, now with a 6 handicap, played for Centaurs.

Casarejo *(Blue, Yellow and white)*
1. Baron Elie de Rothschild (2)
2. R. Gracida (7)
3. A. Gracida (7)
Bk. P. Domecq La Riva (4)

Centaurs *(Blue and yellow)*
1. Dr J. Marin Moreno (6)
2. J.L. Lucas (4)
3. G. Gracida (7)
Bk. E. de Rothschild (2)

The following year was a successful one for the home team, beating Laversine 7-6, and there was an even more satisfactory result in 1962, when Cowdray Park retained the cup in a match which saw them win 8-5 over a Brazilian team, Sao Silvestre.

Paul Withers, captain of the Cowdray Park team

Cowdray Park *(Orange)*	Sao Silvestre *(Red)*
1. Brig. M.A. Baig (5)	1. W. Simohseh (2)
2. B.B. Bethell (3)	2. J.J. Diaz Alberdi (5)
3. P.M. Withers (5)	3. I. Mihanovich (6)
Bk. C.M.T. Smith Ryland (4)	Bk. A. Mihanovich (5)

As it happened, 1962 - 22nd July - was the last time Cowdray Park won the Gold Cup, although they were to reach the final another eleven times, most recently in 1990. Yet *Horse & Hound* considered that 1962 was 'certainly one of the most successful of the many Goodwood Weeks at Cowdray'. It had attracted more players than ever - 104 of them as well as over 150 ponies in addition to the 20 or more resident at Cowdray.

Playing at No. 3 in 1962 was Paul Withers, a young subaltern serving in Aden with the Royal Horse Artillery who had been flown home to join the team. Paul, today captain of Cowdray Park, has led a polo career which epitomises the help given to young, and not particularly wealthy, players at Cowdray Park. When high handicap games started, low-goal players from the area were invited to make up the numbers. The policy, which continues today, notably in the league match series, provided invaluable experience for the 'young entry'; and as the club had decided in Coronation Year, a new generation of players must be encouraged with facilities to play regularly, without breaking the bank.

Stuart Angell, writing in the 1960s, noted 'a young man, a local farmer's son, now with a handicap of 5, one of the highest in the country'. Today, of course, Paul Withers, with a handicap of 6 is one of the leading British players; but even at the end of the 1962 season, an American magazine, *The Chronicle of the Horse,* had recognised his abilities:

The move was upward for 'Young England', i.e players produced since polo restarted after the war. The big ones are Lt Paul Withers, 5 to 6; Major Ronnie Ferguson, 4 to 5; Lord Patrick Beresford, 3 to 4; John Lucas, 4 to 5.

Paul Withers going to 6 goals makes him the highest handicapped British player extant. Considering the fact that this 23-year-old, 6ft 4in tall, ball-busting, block-buster was a minus 1 six years ago, its a considerable feat. As Baron Elie de Rothschild says: 'If he has the opportunity he will be 10 goals in another couple of years.'

Born in 1939, Paul Withers grew up with horses: his father, Fred, was

Lawns, top centre, Cowdray Ruins and the River Ground (centre)

Ambersham Grounds

a tenant farmer on the Cowdray estate, farming 250 acres and running a livery yard. Withers *pere,* who died in 1985, was a keen horseman and hunting man, as his son recalls.

He rode with the Cowdray Hunt and became very friendly with Lord Cowdray, ending up as MFH. He would buy young unmade horses at sales for £70 or £80, make them and play polo on them himself. He was an extremely good horseman, with a good reputation.

Young Paul started to play polo with his father when he left school at seventeen, although in those days cricket was his game - so much so that he was given a trial for the Sussex Colts. Spectators at the annual cricket match organised for friends of Ione O'Brien's Park House Hotel will know that Withers usually lasts longer at the wicket than other polo players; but any thoughts of a cricketing career were forgotten 'when I was bitten by the polo bug!'

Paul Withers waiting to bat at the 1991 Park House match

Leaving school, Paul worked with his father on the farm for a time but then joined the Army on a short service commission of four years.

It had to be the RHA, of course, and I really did nothing but play polo. I had been in the regiment for six months and became an officer. This was rather unprecedented but my Colonel wanted me because I played polo!

In his early days, he was asked to play for the Polo Cottage team of Mike Holden White, based at Easebourne.

Mike couldn't play himself any more but instead of giving up altogether he kept a string of ponies and mounted people as the Polo Cottage team. When he asked if I would play for him it was a present from Heaven! He made me spend a lot of time on the wooden horse and it was really because of him that I began to play properly.

Paul saw the renaissance of polo at Cowdray Park, and he remembers

All eyes on the cricket ball: Charles Seavill, Alan Kent and Oliver Ellis. Below: The Park House teams, 1991, with Ione O'Brien. Paul Withers is fifth from left in the back row

the friendly, intimate, atmosphere - and the fine of 1s. every time a player swore.

We always played on Wednesdays, Thursdays and Fridays. There were a lot of players, although obviously nothing like as many as today, but it was good fun. Of course, I would get as upset as the next man and I had rather a bad reputation on the polo field when I was younger. But I have always lived and breathed polo and when I see some of the unhappy faces in the game today I wonder whether those players should really be playing the sport.

After leaving the Army, Paul Withers joined Lloyd's as an underwriter, but three years of commuting to and from London was too much for him. From 1966 to 1972 he was in the Argentine, but returned to England every season playing for Windsor Park, including 1969 when Windsor defeated Pimms 7-6 in the Gold Cup final.

I turned professional in a minor way in 1973, and then only for a year. Vivyan Naylor-Leyland paid me £1,200 for a season but I had an

Cowdray Park Gold Cup finalists, 1990: Pearson, Ezcurra, Badiola, Withers

unhappy time. My father was in Vivyan's medium-goal team and he wanted to drop him, which I didn't like at all. I presented Vivyan with a cheque for £600 to clear myself with him and then Lord Cowdray asked me to play for him and the stewards ruled in my favour. I was extremely lucky: John Cowdray has been like a Godfather to me, and without him and Mike Holden White I would never have played at all.

The arrival of Argentine players at Cowdray in the early years of the Gold Cup saw standards of play increase still further and, as Withers emphasises, professionalism began to be recognised, despite the fact that many players disliked admitting the fact that they were anything other than amateurs.

In those days you bought their ponies: nowadays you pay them high fees. Of course, the pressure on a professional can be severe, not so much because one is paid and feels that winning is essential, but because as a pro one feels that playing well is important. What I do not like is the behaviour of certain patrons who agree a fee with a player and then offer more if he wins. This is not polo!

The chukka stage of polo is still great fun, but I suppose I was born a competitor. You cannot imagine the depths of depression or extremes of elation if you lose or win, especially if it is a big game. I certainly feel that I owe it to John Cowdray to win, yet while he is overjoyed if Cowdray Park does win a game, or a cup, he is also the best loser possible.

This, too, was the feeling amongst the crowd of over six thousand watching the final of the Gold Cup on The Lawns, Cowdray, on 22nd July, 1990, when Cowdray Park lost 9-10 to the turquoise-shirted Hildon House but only after two extra chukkas. Withers was playing back with Charles Pearson (2) at No. 1, Thomas Ezcurra (6) at No. 2 and Juan Badiola (8) at No. 3. One of the fastest and most exciting games of the season finished with a moment of astonished disbelief for the spectators and the loudest applause was reserved for Lord Cowdray as he finished his short speech of thanks to all the players. Surely the foundations of the ruined Cowdray House moved a little at the cheering. Certainly, few eyes were dry in the grandstand.

Withers has played in thirty countries, including the Argentine, where he recalls up to 40,000 spectators at a match at Palermo, the Mecca of polo.

I have met the most delightful people, and have had the honour of playing in India with Hanut Singh. They had grounds like billiard tables out there - and whippy sticks. Now it is all very different in India, where polo is a subsided game for the 61st Cavalry. It is sad that we can never see an Indian high-goal team over here any more.

Rao Rajah Hanut Singh was very much a part of Cowdray in the 'sixties. His most notable achievement in later life, perhaps, was to win the Gold Cup for Eric Moller's Jersey Lilies in 1964 (when they beat Centaurs 10-3) and again in 1965, with a 9-5 victory over Cowdray Park. Still playing off a handicap of 3 when he retired at the age of seventy-two, Hanut Singh organised the teams with a judgement based on years of experience. Many older club members will also remember his appearance, in a suit of armour borrowed from Cowdray House, in one of the Park House cricket matches.

Indeed, stories about him are legion. Mollie Tatham recalls him staying at Park House, Bepton:

He taught polo at the breakfast table, using salt cellars, mustard and pepper pots as players, showing the young players where to place themselves, where to attack, and so on. Like all Indians who ride, he was a beautiful horseman, with light, kind, hands and he would never pull a pony's mouth about. All the Indian and Pakistani players' ponies always looked happy, with pricked-up ears . . .

Robert de Pass also recalls an amusing anecdote concerning Hanut at Park House.

He always brought his bearer, Sawai, with him. In those days there was only one bathroom at Park House and Sawai would sit cross-legged outside the door so that no other guest could use the bathroom before Hanut.

It was perhaps inevitable that as the Gold Cup tournament attracted more players from more countries, so did the eye of the observers become more critical. In the Gold Cup final of 1963, for example, *The Times* reported 'a stern, battling game with more penalties than one usually expects to see in a top class final.' Cowdray Park had held the cup for two years and this season Alec Harper (5), Paul Withers (6), Sinclair Hill (7) and Charles Smith Ryland (4) faced a South American team, La Vulci, captained by the Italian Marquess Giacinto Guglielmi di Vulci, who played to a 1 in first position.

Cowdray Park led 6-2 at half-time but in the second half, as *The*

Times noted, 'La Vulci's excellent combination and experience began to pay dividends'. The visitors won, 8-7, their first attempt for the Gold Cup. *Horse & Hound* blamed Cowdray's performance in the second half on the absence of Heskie Baig.

Four good players - three backs and a No. 3 of great merit - rather than a well-balanced team, and this time the cracked pot went to the well once too often. Gonzalez (the 6-handicap back for La Vulci) administered the coup de grace with a forty yard penalty. Withers was certainly a tower of strength, and he and Hill are a powerful combination: they should benefit from this rather unhappy defeat. We are obliged to La Vulci for an overdue lesson in team work, clear calling, prompt obedience, splendid covering, quickness on the ball and the proper appreciation of the accurate approach shot, which alone can bring victory in high class polo.

Defeat, and this slightly patronising match report, were offset to a certain extent by the fact that no less than nine teams had entered for the tournament, the highest to that date. There was also compensation in the announcement that Lord Cowdray had received one of only three medals awarded that year by the British Horse Society, in recognition of his work for polo. No-one could really reproach the losing side (as did the Archangels' band in Kipling's tale, 'The Maltese Cat') with cries of 'Ooh, Kafoozalum! Kafoozalum! Kafoozalum!'

The public certainly enjoyed their money's worth, not least through seeing the best of the overseas players competing at Cowdray Park. Stuart Angell recalled:

When the real matches started, horsemanship and hard hitting became a real eye-opener, also the accuracy of the back-hand hitting which astonished even a great number of hardened polo players. The Argentine players were particularly skilled at this . . .

Polo in England, due largely to the Cowdray example, had come a long way from the pre-war days when the American sporting journalist Peter Vischer could write with barely concealed disgust of 'the London polo season unfortunately coinciding with the London social season'.

It means that a hard match is not followed by a leisurely dinner and a cool evening in the country, as it would be in the United States, but by a hurried rush to town, to a dinner that is a social event, perhaps a visit to the theatre or the opera, and then a night-club. It is not easy to concentrate on polo when the ladies have their minds on an entirely different routine of activity.

Really, this is not as far-fetched as it sounds. Not so many years ago the Hurlingham Club had a chance to sell its grounds, which are so well within the limits of London that they can best be reached by subway, for such a big price that a truly fabulous country place could have been built some few miles farther out. But the offer was turned down flat; the officers of Hurlingham and their wives didn't care enough about polo to leave the limits of London under any circumstances.

The war killed Hurlingham as it undermined the polo-playing cavalry regiments. Nowadays, up and coming youngsters come largely through the Pony Club, as did both the highest handicapped English player, Howard Hipwood (9) and his brother, the England captain, Julian (8). While that was some little time ago, the fixing of the National Pony Club Polo Championship at Cowdray Park in early August, some fifteen years ago, means that every year a great deal of talent is concentrated in one place for potential patrons to see. And, as Alec Harper emphasised, even if a young player is introduced to the game at one of the low-goal country clubs, such as Rhinefield, formed in the New Forest in 1935, or Ham, 'they always want to move to Cowdray Park or Windsor'.

Colin Baillieu: Pony Club polo

Colin Baillieu played polo at Cowdray from the late 'fifties until retiring from the game eighteen years ago. He ran a team, Unit Four, which he recalls being 'top of the pops in those days' and also played for Lord Brecknock's Pimms, based at nearby Lodsworth House, and for Cowdray Park.

When I gave up, I was asked

if I would take over Pony Club polo. Charles Pearson was one of the early members, together with Oliver Ellis, the Lucas brothers, Will Roberts and Nicky Evans. It became an enormous success, and Cowdray Park was very good about encouraging them and having youngsters in the teams here. Of course, some boys tend to be led away by the glamour and want to turn professional. Their families can't afford it, or there is no room for them, so despite an enormous effort their hopes of a polo career come to nothing.

A quarter of a century ago, of course, there were no kids playing: it just wouldn't have happened. Now, around 120 Pony Club members and 150 or more ponies come to Cowdray every summer. Pony Club polo has really taken off here because of the tremendous goodwill shown by the polo club. I always think of one story being typical of the youngsters' enthusiasm. I remember a young Will Roberts being reminded by his father that they were going on holiday to the south of France the following week. Will turned to his father and said: 'Oh! Daddy! Can't I be let off the holidays this year?'

Certainly, Pony Club polo is no more expensive than eventing and, with the facilities at Cowdray Park, there is nothing to better it.

Yet, at the same time, Paul Withers, one of the 'Young England' players of the 'sixties, warns that a youngster who rises from the Pony Club ranks to play polo can feel he has cornered success until the day his handicap is raised.

Then the telephone stops ringing and he has no money and no job. For twenty-two years I had a handicap of 7, then it went down to 6 and up to 7 again last year. If I hadn't been working for Lord Cowdray, I would be out of a job now. The best way to make polo your career is to be noticed by a patron who will mount you.

Certainly, the days of highly-paid professionals, something unheard of in those early Gold Cup days, are here to stay. Charles Pearson, chairman of Cowdray Park Polo Club and the third generation of his family to play, admits that foreign patrons will pay over the going rate for players and ponies, which is unhelpful to man and beast.

It hypes up the prices. Some patrons also tend to poach players for enormously inflated prices. But, at the end of the day, you won't get high-goal polo unless the players are paid - after all, they do it for a living -

Charles Pearson: third generation

Terry Hanlon: Voice of Polo

although polo is still one of the few games where professionals and amateurs can play together and be seen by the public. Without the patrons, British or foreign, paying members to be in their teams, it is simply unrealistic to expect a certain standard of polo.

The public, naturally, expect to see a good standard of play, particularly if they know the game; and while after the tumult and the shouting of the Gold Cup, and the departure of the 10 goalers to Deauville, come the lesser tournaments, supported by the low-handicap players who are still the backbone of the game, the very fact that the Gold Cup tournament is top of the high-goal charts means that the very best players must be seen at Cowdray Park. From nine international teams in 1963 to twenty-one in 1991 is undoubtedly an accomplishment in the annals of polo.

Perhaps more than anything, the thirty-five years of the British Open Championships for the Cowdray Park Gold Cup have resulted in a high standard of English polo. Terry Hanlon, well-known to thousands as the 'Voice of Polo', commentating at most of the high-goal matches for the last twenty years, plays to a 1-handicap as well as teaching the game from his Ambersham yard.

When I first came to Cowdray we had lovely club polo, albeit orientated to the Gold cup. In my opinion, we have lost much of the club atmosphere, replaced by the somewhat necessary, but not always pleasant, face of professionalism. It is not the fault of the professional, but of some of the patrons, who want to win at all costs and feel cheated if they lose. Playing cards with friends with no money involved is fun; playing for money is a different game. Yet at the same time the standard of polo here is wonderful, because of the support of the patrons. Having seen it, I find it very difficult to return to 'hit the ball and run' type of game! If you asked me whether I feel I have contributed anything to polo, I would say that I have tried to teach the patrons who have come to me for coaching how to enjoy polo and how to play to the rules - which is what the game is all about. I try to educate the spectators, and as the audiences here have increased out of all recognition over the last two decades, commentating has become far more enjoyable for me, as I hope it has for them.

As polo coach, I hope I am saving men of 40 plus from having heart attacks by pumping the blood round their systems and making them realise that they are not supposed to sit in offices all day. Man should be out hunting food for his family, and polo to me has the same feeling: it is all about the camaraderie of four men playing against four others. It is exhilarating beyond belief!

The camaraderie of Cowdray, particularly in the early years of the Gold Cup, is remembered too by Gayatri Devi, Raj Mata of Jaipur, widow of HH Sir Sawai Man Singh II Bahadur, Maharajah of Jaipur (1911-1970). 'Jai', as he was known to a wide circle of friends (and, behind his back, by those who had social aspirations), was one of the leading Indian polo players: in 1933, before he married the beautiful Cooch Behar princess, he brought his Jaipur team to England, where it set a record by winning all the open tournaments. Later, in 1957, he led the Indian team to victory in the Gold Cup at Deauville.

When we came to Cowdray (recalls the Raj Mata) everybody knew everybody else. My husband and I would stay sometimes at Cowdray House, sometimes with Ione O'Brien at Park House, Bepton, and once we took a cottage at Rogate, up the road from Midhurst.

The leading figures in polo in those days included Sir Rex Benson, who had played polo in the 9th Lancers and who lived at Drovers, near

Above (left): HH The Raj Mata of Jaipur; (right) the Maharajah and Prince Philip after a match at Cowdray Park. Below: The Maharajah of Jaipur prepares for a match at Cowdray Park in 1948

Singleton; Lord Rocksavage (later the 6th Marquess of Cholmondeley),who used to take Cucumber Farm, near Drovers, for the season; Alec Harper at Ambersham and my brother, the Maharajah of Cooch Behar, who played to a 2 and who rented a cottage at Ambersham in the late 1950s, when he gave the high-goal Cooch Behar Cup. Everyone was polo-minded, which is still one of the great attractions at Cowdray, and everyone in the crowd knew you. I can remember standing in the pony lines and members of the public would come up to me and say 'If England can't win so-and-so today, we want the Indians to win - not the Americans!' Spectators at Cowdray were, and are, great followers of the game and they all have their favourite teams. There were crowds for the Gold Cup in the '50s and '60s, although in those days there was only one small stand on the Lawns. Most people would sit on the grass and picnic.*

One wonders about team partisanship on a day such as 10th June, 1957 when India beat Cowdray Park, 8-5 in the final of the Duke of Sutherland Cup.

India *(Light blue)*	Cowdray Park *(Orange)*
1. Capt Kishen Singh (4)	1. Col G.H. Critchley (4)
2. Kunwar Bijai Singh (4)	2. C. Smith Ryland (4)
3. Rao Raja Hanut Singh (6)	3. Lt Col A.F. Harper (5)
Bk. HH The Maharajah of Jaipur (5)	Bk. J. Lakin (6)

Jaipur, who at the height of his career played to a 9 handicap, always regarded polo as a man's game, as the Raj Mata remembers with amusement.

I was late for breakfast once in India and when my husband asked where I had been I said 'On the wooden horse', adding that I was thinking of starting a ladies' team. 'No woman will ever play in my team or on my ground,' said my husband. The next time we came to Cowdray I couldn't help laughing: Daphne Lakin was in my husband's team and her sister, Yoskyl, was in the opposing team. The only woman I can actually remember playing in India was the Nawab of Bhopal's daughter, but she never played abroad.

One would be interested in the Maharajah's comments on the 1992 Cowdray scene, where a promising player for the low-goal Cowdray Park

*Today, Drovers is owned by Brook Johnson, whose Ambersham-based American team, C.S. Brooks, won the Ashton Cup, subsidiary to the Gold cup, in 1991. Appropriately, they also won the Cooch Behar Cup.

team is Sehr Ahmad (-1), the 23-year-old Pakistani ladies' captain. Doubtless the doughty old Indian players would approve, for she follows in the footsteps of her uncle, Brigadier 'Heskie' Baig, who played for the home team in the 1962 Gold Cup victory.

Another change noticed by the Raj Mata is, not unexpectedly, the rise of the professional:

When they started to appear on the scene, they would mix with everyone else. Now, I believe, they stick to each other. Of course, in the early days of the Gold Cup, the professionals were invaluable for high-goal matches. Patrons such as Lord Cowdray, Eric Moller and Arthur Lucas were sensible, playing low- and medium-goal polo and sticking within their limits, using their pros for high-goal games. Unfortunately, some patrons coming into the scene later tried to play beyond their abilities and, as a result, ruined the teams.

To many followers of polo at Cowdray, ponies in the '50s and '60s, especially those from the Indian teams, were much faster than today, even when compared with the Argentine mounts.

They were magnificent (recalls Brian Bethell); we had very fast polo then. The Indians never tended to slow up, as the South Americans will often do nowadays in the middle of a game. I can remember all their equipment would be laid out on the side of the ground on blankets, with their Indian stick makers in attendance.

Certainly the Jaipur team, accustomed to playing before crowds of 100,000 in Calcutta, deserved the adulation accorded them by polo writers before and after the last war. 'Extraordinary ability . . . ' 'miraculous force . . . ' 'can rise to an emergency . . . ' were phrases that followed the Maharajah and his team around the world.

As Brian Bethell noted, ponies helped. A favourite pony of the Maharajah was Drake, a bay bred by the Queen and ridden by Prince Philip at Cowdray Park. The Jaipurs, unable to find a house close to Cowdray - much to the Raj Mata's lasting regret - had taken a place at Ascot:

Drake came to our stables, which were run by Judy Balding. My husband was extremely fond of Drake and one day I decided to buy the pony as a birthday present for him. At first my husband was appalled: 'What on earth have you done? You don't know anything about horses. How much did you pay for him?' He imagined that I paid way over the top, of course, but when I told him that Drake had cost me £400 he gave me the most enormous hug! Drake became his best pony and when my husband died during a polo match at Cirencester, nobody else could play him. I retired Drake to stables in Norfolk.

Over the years, of course, many ponies have captured the public imagination at Cowdray Park, the reigning champion being Chesney, from David Jamison's Westerlands Stud, of whom more later. A pony long remembered was Dinna Peep, Lord Cowdray's grey mare, born in 1966 with a hole in her heart. Brenda Freeling recalls the girl grooms had to milk the dam, Wee Din, by rote; but Dinna Peep went on to play polo well into the 1970s before retiring honourably. Her name appeared every season in the list of ponies published in the Cowdray programme, a feature possible in the days of smaller pony lines. Robert de Pass, who played for Prince Philip's Mariners team in the early 1950s and, later, for Sir Vivyan Naylor-Leyland's Martyrs, remembers how few ponies played in the initial days of the Gold Cup.

The final would be played over five chukkas with a handicap limit of, say, 20. The players would perhaps have up to six ponies: nowadays, the sky's the limit, although few people could compete with someone like Kerry Packer!

Lt Cmdr de Pass first played polo at Rhinefield, the New Forest club, in 1947, then with Lord Mountbatten in Malta, before moving to New Grove, Petworth, in 1955.

We bred ponies at New Grove for years. I remember one in particu-

Tarquin, with groom Mervyn Barnes, 1970

lar, Tarquin, bred from Gay Presto out of Taquara. He was borrowed by Paul Withers when he went to the Argentine and won the prize for the best heavyweight over there in 1966 - and again at Deauville in 1971. I went on riding him until he was 28 or so. In the '50s, most of the polo ponies here came from the Argentine, although quite a few were bought in from pony racing stables for £150 to £200, although it took another two years to train them for polo.

Robert de Pass retired from the polo field, with a handicap of 2, at the beginning of the '70s, having seen the game at Cowdray develop dramatically.

One of the biggest changes has been the rise of the professional. Up until 1968 or even 1970 one might have seen a single pro in each high goal team. This has altered, which is a good thing for the game. After all, the proof of the pudding is the way in which polo has spread and grown as a sport, although it is heinously expensive, especially for youngsters who, even if they have the time and the money to turn professional, find themselves up against two 9 or 10 handicap Argentinians.

A major change, as far as the Gold Cup is concerned, came in 1977 when a league system was introduced. Initially, there were two leagues of six teams (today, there are four leagues) with the top team in each league playing each other for the Gold Cup, the seconds for the Midhurst Town Cup, presented by the local Chamber of Commerce; the thirds for the Jack Gannon Trophy, the fourths for the Tatham Cup, presented by Lord Cowdray in memory of polo manager 'Bolshie' Tatham. Since the introduction of the system, Gold Cup Winners have been Foxcote, 1977; Stowell Park 1978 and 1980; Songhai 1979; Falcons 1981 and 1983; Southfields 1982 and 1984; Maple Leafs 1985; Tramontana 1986 to 1989 and 1991; Hildon House 1990. Cowdray Park were runners-up on six occasions.

Throughout the polo-playing world, the Cowdray Park Gold Cup is 'still the one people want to win', and 'the one into which they throw everything,' says David Jamison, whose Westerlands Stud, at Graffham near Ambersham, produces some of the best ponies (and players) in the world. Jamison first played at Cowdray Park, with a 0 handicap, in 1977 with his team Chopendoz. In 1980 he started high-goal polo, four years later becoming joint player-patron with David Yeoman, their Southfield team beating Cowdray Park in the Warwickshire Cup at Cirencester and Christian Heppe's BBs, 9-2, in the Gold Cup at Cowdray.

We won the three Englishmen, which I'd always wanted to do (David Jamison recalls). The team was David Yeoman (3), Alan Kent (7), Owen Rinehart, now captain of America (7) and myself at Back with a 3 handicap.

David Jamison, master of Westerlands

It was a major victory for what, as *The Times* reported, was 'one of the best balanced and most effective polo combinations seen on English grounds since the last war'. The following year, 1985, the Jamison-Yeoman combination put together Centaurs, recalling Evelyn de Rothschild's Gold Cup winners; and whether as Southfields or Centaurs, the team was seen generally as one of the most successful in British high-goal polo since the post-war revival. Jamison also made a name as captain of the Singapore team, but it was in 1987 that he joined forces, again as a player-patron, with Anthony Embiricos, a team described by *Country Life* as, simply, the best in England.

The architect of Tramontana's record success in the Gold Cup has always been Carlos Gracida, 'a demi-god . . . the fastest and most nimble man on the British polo field' as he has been called. The third generation of his family to play polo, the 10-handicap Mexican and his brother, Memo, now an American citizen, looked to their grandfather for inspiration.

He could teach horses jumping, dressage, tricks like rearing up and lying down. In fact the only thing he could not teach them was to talk. My father followed him, and Memo. We lived for horses and polo, which has everything: horsemanship, teamwork, speed and danger.

The team name, from the Greek wind, sums up admirably their success in five Gold Cup finals: 11-4 in 1986, 9-5 in 1987, 15-8 in 1988, 13-8 in 1989 and 11-7 in 1991. And for the last three Tramontana victories the award for the best playing pony went to David Jamison's Chesney, ridden by Carlos Gracida. Chesney, an eight-year-old black gelding, won on the racetrack before being bought for Jamison by David Morley at Ascot Sales in 1986; and he was introduced to low, and then medium-goal polo during the following year. It is not difficult to understand why Jamison turned down an offer of £200,000 for the pony two years ago.

Above: Carlos Gracida, the Mexican 'demi-god'
Below: Memo Gracida in conversation with Brian Bethell

Chesney, David Jamison's celebrated black gelding, with Patrick Churchward (left) and David Morley

Although David Jamison now prefers to play high-goal polo with his Lodsworth team in the USA - 'I can hit the ball there more than three times and I don't find myself up against 10 handicap South American players - he still regards Cowdray Park as the home of European polo.

In one way the atmosphere at Cowdray has been broken up by the number of satellite grounds, which were required due to the number of players: myself at Westerlands, Kerry Packer at Stedham, Alan Kent at Madam's Farm, Midhurst, for instance. But high-goal polo will always be centred within the Cowdray Park area. This year (1991) the Gold Cup had the finest ponies on one ground anywhere in the world.

Anthony Embiricos, patron of Tramontana, five times winners of the Gold Cup

Over the years, David Jamison, now a valued member of the Cowdray Park Polo Club committee, has seen the game grow in popularity as a spectator sport.

But at the same time I don't think the style is quite what it was. I'm trying to create, perhaps re-create, a country house polo atmosphere, playing on friends' grounds in the area and holding barbecues afterwards. I want to see 'fun' polo again as a counterbalance to the amount of finance that has come in. I just hope that in five years time corporation money does not ruin the greatest sport in the world.

Despite inevitable changes - greater sums of money involved, more ponies, an extension of the season among them - the essential atmosphere of Cowdray remains, especially to people such as the Raj Mata of Jaipur.

I don't really know many clubs besides Cowdray and Guards, but I do know that even the International Day at Guards cannot come up to the atmosphere at Cowdray Park. People still come down here to watch polo, not to be 'seen' or to stare at well-known faces. Thank God!

The Raj Mata who, as Maharani, entered the *Guinness Book of Records* in 1961 when she won the Jaipur seat in the Indian general election with 157,692 votes out of a total of 192,000, remains a familiar figure at Cowdray Park. Indeed, she may still hold a record yet to appear in the Guinness annals: she was the sole spectator at the end of a game on the River Ground in the 1960s. It was during Goodwood Week, when matches begin traditionally at 4.30 pm, rather than 3 pm, and the game was still in full swing at 8 pm.

CHUKKA FIVE

Players and Ponies

West Sussex, that last stronghold of Old England, comes into its own for a week at the end of July . . . In August we return to our 18th century privacy and primitive ways . . . (*The Sphere*, July 1948)

This quotation from a faded cutting in Daphne Lakin's photograph album referred obviously to Goodwood Week polo at Cowdray Park, rather than the Gold Cup tournament. Yet it remains true, over forty years on, in the sense that there is an almost tangible relaxation at Cowdray once Gold Cup Day is over. There is still one high goal match to play - the Cowdray Park Challenge Cup - in early August, and there is the exuberance of the National Pony Club Championships, which have come to Cowdray in August for the last fifteen years, to face; but there is also the 'good polo' of low and medium tournaments to enjoy until mid-September: the Harrison, Aotea, Maidensgrove, the new Autumn Cup, all in the medium league, and the Holden White, Ruins, Brecknock, West Sussex and Farewell cups for low-handicap players.

A feature once again of the second half of the season is the American tournament which, if played on the favourite River Ground, provides the newcomer among the spectators with a brilliant exposition of the game. Robert de Pass recalls:

I played in an American tournament in 1953. Basically, it was a means of giving twelve people four chukkas of good polo each; we had three teams of four players, each match to last for two chukkas. It gave people who might not otherwise have a game the chance to play against everyone else.

The first such tournament recorded in the Cowdray scorebook took place on Whit Monday, 25th May, 1953 in what has gone down for posterity as being 'perfect sunshine'. The first two chukkas were played between the green-shirted Mixed Grill (Lt Cmdr R.E.F. de Pass, 0; W. Warner Boulton, 2; Cmdr L. Farmer, 2 and Lt Col D. de C. Smiley, 0) and the red-shirted Colts (Capt W.D.A. Bagnell, -1; Col S.W. Harris, 2; Lt Col D.F.G. Smith, 1 and Capt J. MacDonald-Buchanan, 1). Colts won by 3½-1. The next two chukkas resulted in a 4½-2 win over Mixed Grill by Cowdray Park (Lord Cowdray, 1; Lt Col C.G.N. Turner, 0; Hon Mrs J. Lakin, 0 and HRH The Duke of Edinburgh, 2); and in the final match, Prince Philip having been replaced by the 3-handicap Harold Freeborn, Cowdray Park beat Colts by 2-½.

Until comparatively recently, of course, matches were held at Cowdray Park only at weekends, with chukkas on Wednesdays and Fridays. Major Ronnie Ferguson, now polo manager to the Prince of Wales,

Lt Cmdr Robert de Pass

Major Ronnie Ferguson

started playing the game as a young Army officer in the mid-1950s and, through his father's friendship with John Lakin, was offered a trial at Cowdray. It did not bode well for his future in polo.

Lord Cowdray told me that I would never be a polo player and said that I hit the ball like a squash player. It was the end of my trial here, but I nevertheless managed to end up with a handicap of 5 and played as a visitor, with the Windsor Park team, at Cowdray until the end of my active career.

Major Ferguson later worked with Lord Cowdray, then chairman of the HPA, as a steward and as chief umpire and, despite the initial setback, stresses the debt owed by the polo world to him.

There is no one in polo who isn't grateful to John Cowdray. The revival of the game after the war is due to him. Of course, if he hadn't resurrected polo, someone else might have done; but the fact remains that it was John Cowdray who did it. Over the last thirty-seven years I have always had the greatest fun at Cowdray Park.

It was fun that once very nearly turned into tragedy. In one Cowdray Challenge Cup final, Major Ferguson, riding his grey mare Novara, was pushed into the goal post by another player. Remounting, he continued to play until, suddenly, his left side became paralysed.

I then discovered that I had actually broken my neck, and I was out of action for six months. It didn't deter me, however, and, in my memory, the accident is eliminated by the fact that I was three times in Lord Brecknock's Pimms team when they won the Gold Cup - in 1968, 1971 and 1972.

Johnnie Kidd will be familiar to many people as the former international showjumper - he was, among other victories, European Junior Champion in 1962. Today, his Holders team is one of many based in the

Two generations of polo players: Johnnie Kidd (right) and his son, Jack

Cowdray Park area (although, technically, it is the Barbados Polo Club team), but when he first played here in the early 1970s, Cowdray was the centre of what he recalls as a 'classical, amateur, sport'.

When I left showjumping, polo was amateur in the sense that one worked at a job during the week and played polo at weekends. Chukkas were played on a Friday, always at 5 pm, so that those of us working in London could join the POETS Society - Piss Off Early, Tomorrow's Saturday - and drive down in time for chukkas.

In those days, too, the number of ponies owned by, or available to, the average player was much lower than today. Kidd, as he made the transition from showjumping to polo, had two mounts who would be 'double-chukkered' and remembers one occasion when he used one pony for three chukkas in a final of the Harrison Cup.

I also remember in particular Farmer, a grey, which I bought from Sandy Harper for £200 and a crate of champagne. He was famous for his enormous size and I played him for several seasons. I even put my son, Jack, then aged 12 or 13, up on him because he was so big and safe. Eventually I decided that Farmer must go to the knacker's yard. I was away at the time, and when I returned I discovered that my groom, who was very upset at my decision, had sold Farmer to someone living locally who just wanted a horse to ride. I learned recently that, at the age of twenty-three, Farmer has just won his first showjumping competition!

Kidd played initially for the Todham team, where team-mates included Ronnie Driver, Julian Hipwood and Robert de Pass. In 1975 he joined Eric Moller's Jersey Lilies and the following year won the Cowdray Park Challenge Cup, 13-7½. Over the years, Kidd has won every tournament apart from the Gold Cup, and 1991 proved especially memorable for him: Holders, in a final for the first time, won the new Autumn Cup.

The Todham team eventually became San Flamingo and a fellow-player of Johnnie Kidd there, and subsequently with Jersey Lilies, was Alan Kent, now a 7 handicap player and very much a part of the Cowdray Park scene.

Like so many contemporary players, Kent enjoyed his first taste of the game with the Pony Club, in this case the New Forest branch, during his prep-school years, before going to Millfield, then the only public school

From Alan Kent's scrapbook. Top: The 1974 San Flamingo team with (centre) American polo enthusiast Bill Ylvisaker: Alan Kent, Howard Hipwood, Ronnie Driver and Julian Hipwood. Below: Earl Mountbatten presented the 1979 Gold Cup to Songhai, shortly before his murder in Ireland. From left: Oliver Ellis, Songhai patron Ahmadu Yakubu and his son, David; Lord Cowdray, Mrs Yakubu, Alan Kent and Alvaro Pieres. Note the Kent beard . . .

with a real polo team.

I was hooked on polo from an early age, although originally I found point-to-pointing rather more fun. But as long as it involved horses it got me out of my prep school gates!

Later, Kent played for Rhinefield, the New Forest club which has sent so many notable players to Cowdray Park. There he met Phil Rhodes and Patrick Churchward (today the veterinary surgeon for David Jamison's Westerlands Stud) who invited him to play at Cowdray in Rhodes's low-goal Carvers team.

I think I had a handicap of 1 then. I spent a couple of years with Carvers, but at the time didn't particularly want to turn professional. I was living the life of Riley: driving up to Cowdray at the weekends, working a stud during the week and point-to-pointing in the winter. I must say that Carvers was a very successful team: we lost only one game in my first season with them.

Moving to the medium-goal San Flamingo, Kent spent a happy season living in a caravan at Heyshott. Julian Hipwood, who retired as captain of England at the end of the 1991 season, remembers 'this long-haired youth on a battered old motorcycle with a couple of polo sticks held between his legs'. Hipwood and Johnnie Kidd 'sneaked' Kent into Jersey Lilies. He remained there for two or more seasons, playing low, high and medium goal, although he recalls that in his first high-goal season he hardly hit the ball.

Relaxing: Julian Hipwood and Alan Kent

By 1979 Kent was in the Gold Cup final with Songhai, that year's winners.

Three years later he was with David Jamison's Southfields when they won the same trophy; but what he regards as one of his 'greatest honours' was when he was asked to play for Cowdray Park in the 1991 season.

Like Johnnie Kidd, Alan Kent recalls no weekday finals, or any major games apart from weekends, during his early days at Cowdray Park. But if Wednesday and Friday were reserved for chukkas, there was hard work for the aspiring professional as Julian Hipwood remembers.

I first came to Cowdray in 1963 or 1964 and stayed at Park House, Bepton. Hanut Singh picked the Jersey Lilies team in those days and he brought me here. I was 17 or 18 at the time and it was Hanut who got me into the game. He used to make me get up at five in the morning and we would go off to the River Ground stables. Then it was across to the House Ground where Hanut would make me trot - never canter or gallop - until it was time to go back for breakfast at Park House. After breakfast we went off to Cowdray House, where I would practice on the wooden horse. Hanut gave me £5 a week pocket money and I was not allowed to go out at night. It was hard work - but worth it!

Hipwood went from a handicap of 0 to 6 in his first six years at Cowdray Park. He joined the home team for two seasons in 1969 and, since then, has missed only one season at the club.

Like Paul Withers, Hipwood did not select polo at his first sport. In his youth he wanted to become a professional footballer and played in the second team for his local club, Bristol Rovers.

When I was young I would play football and polo at the weekends; polo with the VWH Pony Club and my brother, Howard. But when I came to Cowdray I quickly learned one thing: Cowdray Park is not just a polo club, it is an institution. The atmosphere in the '60s and '70s was marvellous. Any game is competitive but, certainly in those days, it was not the end of the world if your team didn't win a game. Winning should be important, but it seems now as though 90 per cent of polo players take part to win, only 10 per cent because of the fun. I always remember Hanut Singh telling me, if I lost a match, to go straight into the bar and talk to people - to show that I could be a good loser.

Someone who readily admits that she plays simply for fun is Lavinia Black, today one of the three lady players out of a playing membership of

103 at Cowdray. Mrs Black, who has played in nearly a dozen countries, began polo in the Pony Club - in fact, Pony Club polo was initiated by her father, Alan Roberts, and Sarah Williams.

My father had a handicap of 3 and started the Henley Polo Club, playing with Archie David, who was my Godfather. We went to Rhodesia for a time and then, when I was about 17, came back to England and bought a farm at Graffham. My father said that I would have to play polo, or he wouldn't keep my pony, but I really became hooked on the game a couple of years later, when I went to stay in the Argentine with the Marin Morenos (Jorge Marin Moreno was in the Los Indios team which won the

Lavinia Black and her collection of autographs of 4-handicap players and above at Cowdray Park, made over the last twenty years

first Gold Cup in 1956.) That was it: if you stay in a polo-playing country you are expected to play polo and events came to me in a natural sequence after that.

I've been a 2 handicap for more than 20 years and I've played for nearly every team you can think. Its been great fun going around the various clubs and I'm certainly not interested in the money aspect of the game.

Mrs Black played for Jersey Lilies - 'with that long-haired youth, Alan Kent' - and for Maidensgrove, the team formed by her father and remembered now in the medium goal Maidensgrove cup tournament, the quarter finals for which begin the weekend after the Gold Cup final. The team was named after two successive houses owned by the Roberts family, at Henley and in Rhodesia.

And, like Johnnie Kidd with his grey Farmer, Mrs Black had a favourite pony, the English thoroughbred Binney.

I had Binney as a yearling and made him at Graffham. Paul Withers borrowed him for two years to play in the International and now, at the age of twenty five, my 12-year-old son, Alastair, plays him.

Young Alastair Black is the third generation of yet another Cowdray Park family and has just gone to Wellington College where, under the auspices of the recently-formed Schools Polo Association, a new club has been launched.

Lavinia Black always looks forward to the relaxed atmosphere, that 18th century privacy, of the season once the Gold Cup is over. Only the parties are missing.

In the old days everyone gave a party. My father found it very hard to hold our own party - there was rarely a night free. Today, the professionals don't like going to parties - it might affect their game the next day.

Mrs Black is very much in the mould of the polo-playing Pearson sisters, Yoskyl, Angela and Daphne, although she has played in the Argentine, which Daphne Lakin, visiting after the last war, discovered to be *de trop,* and, once, in a high-goal match at Cowdray Park. Unwittingly, she broke an unwritten rule that women did not play at so elevated a level.

Clare Tomlinson (daughter of the celebrated Arthur Lucas and, at 3, the highest handicapped woman player in England) and I thought enough was enough. We actually threatened to take Cowdray Park to the Equal Opportunities Commission. The club backed down but, because of the inherently friendly nature of Cowdray, we both still play here . . .

The West Sussex Cup, a low-goal tournament held at the end of August, epitomises the 18th century spirit of Cowdray Park. By a coincidence, Brigadier Arthur Douglas-Nugent, polo manager at Cowdray for the last two seasons, came to the club first in the summer of 1957 as a visiting player.

I was in the 17/21 Lancers, stationed in Germany, and had played polo since I joined the regiment in 1953. We always regarded ourselves as the most famous polo regiment, having won the Open for 10 years on the trot, from 1920 to 1930. We came to Cowdray as the BAOR Colts. I can remember that Lord Cowdray had bought ponies from the New Zealand

Polo manager Arthur Douglas-Nugent: relaxing (left) and in action on the polo ground at Ambersham playing No. 1 for Sonali

team, Aotea, and he rented them to invited visitors. We were a very enthusiastic team and coming to Cowdray Park was a great event for us.

The red and blue Colts with the then Capt Douglas-Nugent (1) beat

Mike Holden White's Polo Cottage $8^{1}/_{2}$-2 in the semi-finals of the West Sussex Cup on 24th August that year. In the final, the following weekend, they lost 3-6 to Pirates. Little did the young captain think that, over thirty years later, he would be working at Cowdray Park.

Arthur Douglas-Nugent was fortunate in that, in his early days in the Army, there were several officers who had played in the halcyon days in India. As they retired, polo 'fizzled out in the Army and soldiering became far more of a profession'.

In my day, the Army was more fun, I suppose. We never thought of the promotion side and, in my regiment at least, one had to own a horse before a car. We were lucky because we had a lot of ponies captured in Italy during the war and trained as polo ponies.

Douglas-Nugent ran the Rhine Army Polo Club in the late '50s before becoming manager of the Lagos Polo Club and then, for the first time as a professional, moving to the Dominican Republic as manager of the Casa de Campo, a Caribbean paradise where polo was introduced by Maharajah Jabar Singh, an 8-handicap player who died in 1986. Arthur Douglas-Nugent took up his new post in the same year, discovering the 'only place in the world where one can play polo by credit card'.

When 'Bolshie' Tatham retired at the end of the 1976 season, the post of polo manager at Cowdray was advertised in *Horse & Hound.* Arthur Douglas-Nugent saw it and applied, as did a great many other people including the late, irrepressible, Col Hilary Hook, who became something of an institution following a documentary on his life shown on television. In the event, Peter Cruden followed in Col Tatham's footsteps, while Douglas-Nugent had in fact withdrawn his application.

The Dominican Republic was keen to introduce Europeans to polo there. In 1988 I went to Deauville and happened to meet Paul Withers, whom I had known in the past. He told me that Peter Cruden was going to retire and suggested I apply for the job again. I still couldn't make up my mind, thinking it would take five years to achieve anything in the Dominican Republic; but eventually I applied and was finally interviewed in the autumn of 1988. I was accepted.

To Arthur Douglas-Nugent, Cowdray Park 'means polo for polo's sake - of all the serious clubs in Britain, Cowdray Park and Cirencester have achieved this.'

It is important to make polo as enjoyable as possible, at the same time maintaining the standards of Cowdray Park, which sometimes might result in a compromise. But we are extremely privileged to hold the British Open Championship year after year here-there is no doubt that it is the premier European Championship.

Oliver Ellis

In 1970, long before 'Bolshie' Tatham contemplated retirement, 16-year-old Oliver Ellis, living then at Barlavington Manor, near Petworth, was chosen to play indoor polo for the Great Britain Pony Club for a fortnight in the USA. His side won against Cornell and Harvard but lost to teams from OxRidge and Yale.

Oliver Ellis, who six years later Sinclair Hill was to call 'the best young English prospect', also began his polo career with the Pony club, this time the Cowdray branch.

There were two boys and hundreds of girls (he recalls) and we were suddenly offered polo in the afternoon curriculum. Lord Cowdray leant us a couple of ponies - and I was hooked.

Today, Ellis, with a handicap of 5, is among seventeen Cowdray Park players to rank among the thirty-four leading British players. For most of the '70s he played low goal polo with Mike Holden White's Polo Cottage team - 'Mike was the first person to make me take up the game seriously' - and then medium goal with Paul Withers's Heath Lodge, winning the Smith's Lawn Cup at Windsor in 1973.

I started to play professionally in 1978 with Songhai, winning the Gold Cup the following year, and I was in the final with Ipanema in 1981, when we lost 3-13 to Falcons. My handicap by then was 5 and it seemed the only way to continue playing was to build up my own horses.

Today, Ellis keeps between fifteen and twenty ponies and, he admits, he exists because of them.

Your ponies make you a living. Polo is such an extraordinary game, really, but you can make a living, however precarious it may seem at times.

Like many another young player, he had only a few ponies in his early days at Cowdray Park and the need to conserve their energy was paramount. A favourite has always been Laura, 'a very small and straight mare', which he has owned for the last ten years. Ellis has stables and a yard at Hoyle Farm, Heyshott, which he rents from Colin Baillieu, the former Unit Four patron.

About the time that Sinclair Hill was recognising Oliver Ellis's potential, Nicky Evans was playing polo with Cowdray Pony Club. Nicky, who has a 4 handicap and also features among the top English players, is very much part of a Cowdray polo dynasty: his great-grandfather was 'Bunny' Mathew-Lannowe, who had helped Harold Cowdray revive polo after the Great War.

I first played at Cowdray in 1974, when I was 12 (recalls Nicky). My first chukka was played on ponies hired from Alec Harper. I played Pony Club polo up until 1981 or 1982 and then went into low-goal with Maidensgrove. My big break came in 1979 in Centaurs when, with Alan Kent, Alfonso Pieres and David Jamison, we won the Harrison Cup. For a little kid who'd not played that much it was splendid! I'd decided by then that I was going to be a 10 goaler. I've just learned that, for the 1992 season my handicap has gone down to 4 . . .

Nicky and Lulu Evans

From 1982 until 1990 Evans played low and medium goal with Richard Guess's Rowleys team, based at the old Easebourne Priory stables on the edge of Cowdray Park.

In 1990 he had the chance to play with two of his childhood heroes, Pupi D'Angieri (1) and the 10-goaler Ernesto Trotz, when he was selected as Back for the

Diamond D team in the Gold Cup.

The semi-finals saw us beaten by Cowdray Park. We were literally down to two and a half ponies each, but Cowdray had a borrowing ability greater than our's.

Nevertheless, on Gold Cup Day, 22nd July, Diamond D beat Pendell, 8-7, to win the subsidiary Davidoff Trophy.

Like all the present generation of Cowdray players, Evans has one particular pony recalled with affection. In his case it is Moccasin, bought in from the Argentine by Sinclair Hill.

My father, John Evans, a well-known jump jockey who played polo with Hanut Singh until he broke his back in a racing accident, used to keep a certain Argentinian player's ponies for the winter. Part of the bill was paid with Moccasin and he proved a marvellous starter for me and my brother, Vivian. He had broken down and everyone said that we would never get him sound again. We used him for sixteen months as a lead for young racehorses my father was training and this hardened his leg off. I started playing him in 1976 and carried on until 1983 when Vivian took him over. He was retired for two years when, sadly, we put him to sleep: he was at least twenty years old by then.

When Nicky Evans started playing in Pony Club polo the Cowdray team - himself, William Roberts, David Blunt and Alex Mason - proved invincible for years, winning the championship, which in those days alternated between Cowdray Park and Cirencester, several times. One year, the final went into extra time and it was Moccasin who rose to the occasion when he had to play two chukkas.

Nicky's grandmother, Susan Maxwell, daughter of 'Bunny' Mathew-Lannowe, has been a considerable influence in his polo career and, in his early days, he stabled his ponies in her converted garages. His current yard, at Highstanding, on the Ambersham road from Midhurst, includes sixteen boxes let to Jonathan Wade, one half of the polo-playing Wade twins from Iping.

The best made ponies in the world are from Moccasin's home, the Argentine, according to Cowdray polo coach and commentator Terry Hanlon.

When I started to play I tried to make English horses into polo ponies because the Argentinians were so expensive. But it became an impossible financial equation because at the end of the day it proved far more expensive. Ponies from the Argentine are made to a pattern - there is a technique passed down from father to son. Of course, you can make good ones out of English thoroughbreds if their temperament is right; but if one could send New Zealand thoroughbreds to the Argentine to be mated, you would really have the best polo ponies in the world. I would say that the ideal size is 15.1, at least as far as I'm concerned, and also because the current fashion is for a long polo stick.

A soldier at a later date than Arthur Douglas-Nugent, Charles Fraser, who is married to Lord Cowdray's daughter, Lucy, had none of the problems of taking a horse of his own to Germany, when he joined the Life Guards. A third generation polo player (his grandfather was the 8-handicap Lt Col Sir Denholm Fraser, a name long-remembered in the Indian Army) young Fraser volunteered for his regimental polo team.

When I went to Sandhurst in 1980 I could hit a ball, but by then polo was no longer part of life at the college. The Life Guards, however, were one of the few regiments with a relatively strong team and there was also a very good pool of Army horses in Germany - in any case, because of postings it didn't make sense to have one's own ponies.

Fraser was in the Army for six years but played at Cowdray for the first time four years ago, when he married.

I went from 0 to 2 in one season at Cowdray, playing low-goal with Frasers and medium-goal with Gordon Roddick's Bodyshop. With Frasers, we even reached the final of the Archie David Cup.

For the last two seasons Fraser has played to a 2 handicap with the orange shirts of Cowdray Park: indeed the combination of himself and his brother-in-law, Charles Pearson - the 'two Charles' as they have become known to spectators - can prove intimidating to the opposition. But Fraser's principle is primarily to have a good

Charles Fraser, in Johnnie Kidd's Holders colours

team, made up of players who take part for fun. Now sharing a yard at Great Todham, on the edge of Ambersham, with Julian Hipwood, he says:

If someone asks me to join his team, and I like him and the other players, I'll join them. Cowdray Park is really the nicest club in England: it is rural, there is no hype and we play with the friendliest people. Of course, it is not as it must have been ten years ago, when polo was played mainly for fun and for the parties in the evening, which is how we played in the Life Guards. Since the professionals arrived in the 1980s, and playing membership expanded, the sportsmanship quality is not always there, yet while some of the old atmosphere has, inevitably, gone, there is still something very special about Cowdray Park; and that is all due to Lord Cowdray.

Richard Guess: in the stables of Prioress Elizabeth

A modern player-patron who plays 'purely for enjoyment' is Richard Guess, another 2-goaler in the 1991 season whose white-shirted Rowleys team is named after his well-known restaurant in Jermyn Street. He has played low, medium and high goal polo and, in keeping with the old spirit of Cowdray Park, cares little about winning or losing.

After all, there can be only one Gold Cup winner. I find it fun to play with all sorts of people and, I must admit, one of the things I like about Cowdray is that I can play on a Wednesday and be in my office on a Thursday. I have played in the USA, Brazil and Spain, but, so often abroad, one plays on a Wednesday and twiddles one's fingers for the rest of the week!

Guess began his polo career at Cowdray Park from Terry Hanlon's yard over twelve years ago, and pays tribute to the coach whose pupils have included current patrons Colin Emson, Gordon Roddick, Lord Milford Haven, Mark Franklin, Guy Farley and Garth Bearman, besides Guess himself. Hanlon, says Guess, has been instrumental in developing the club to its present level.

For the last three years Richard Guess has based his ponies at the Priory stables, in the shadow of the old home of the 15th century Prioress Elizabeth, ordered by the Bishop of Chichester to be 'rightly content' with four horses. Today, in the reconditioned stables, there is room for sixteen mounts, including Lucy, ridden by Guess for eight or nine years and still going strong at fifteen, although ready for retirement. For five years, the Priory stables have been under the supervision of groom Sarah Hye, to whom Richard Guess attributes much of his success.

You simply cannot play polo without good grooms. People like me work in London and turn up here to play, but it is the grooms who work long hours in the season and who take the ultimate responsibility for the ponies. Young girls in their 20s taking charge of ponies worth up to £15,000 each do a marvellous job.

In the old days, the hunting season followed polo but, according to Richard Guess, today perhaps three per cent of polo players make the once-natural transition and maintain their stables during the winter months.

If you have a good groom, you cannot lay her off in the winter - it is not fair. I play polo with Terry Hanlon all through the winter - I think there was only one day in the winter of 1990/91 when snow prevented us - and arena or indoor polo also extends the season, at least as far as the grooms and ponies are concerned. I close my yard at the end of the Cowdray season for a while, so that everyone can have a rest, but I keep a couple of ponies at the Cowdray House stables, because we are always trying them out and thinking ahead to the next season.

Richard Guess has known the Cowdray area far longer than he has played polo there. A keen golfer and cricketer, he is devoted to this corner of West Sussex and, from the polo point of view, considers Cowdray Park to be synonymous with the game.

John Cowdray has tried hard to retain the relaxed atmosphere, despite the immense growth in the sport, and the emergence of the professionals. Nowadays, the game is ruled by the professional, rather than the patron or the amateur, but I have played at all the English clubs and Cowdray is still the best for me.

In Brenda Freeling's time as head groom at Cowdray, the Priory was one of the estate stables, with ponies rented out to visiting players. Her successor in the Cowdray House yard, Jackie Wright, arrived in 1974 and, to her, one of the most apparent changes has been in the ponies themselves.

They have become that much finer in my time here. There are far more Latin-bred horses coming into the UK, although we do still have the occasional English thoroughbred in the stable.

As we have seen, every player has his, or her, favourite pony: to Jackie Wright there has only been 'one horse in my lifetime'. He is Archie, Paul Withers's English-Argentine dark bay.

Archie came to Paul aged about three months - he is now 17 - and Paul, Sheldon, his wife, and I have all been involved in making him into a first-class polo pony. To begin with, we never thought that he would carry Paul's weight but over the years he matured and improved. In 1980, at the age of six, he won the award for Best Playing Pony in the Queen's Cup. You can imagine how proud we all were.

Paul Withers is convinced that Archie is 'virtually human':

He does his best for six minutes of a chukka and then goes completely lame. He hobbles off the field but once he has crossed the line walks completely normally. He is a thinking pony and loves every minute of a game, although he flatly refuses to play for more than those six minutes.

Archie was bred by Lord Patrick Beresford and is a prime example of

Archie, with Paul and Sheldon Withers and (left) Cowdray head groom Jackie Wright in the 19th century stableyard at Cowdray House

a pony suiting his rider to perfection. There is an old tradition in polo that success is due 75 per cent to a horse, 25 per cent to a rider. Jackie Wright, who Paul Withers regards as the best polo groom in the world, believes that the percentage is higher, and in favour of the horse.

With the game being so much more competitive today, the pressure on pony and player is much greater. Ponies are used a lot harder now, even in chukkas, and people are looking for the best from every animal. Paul Withers is undoubtedly one of the best riders for his ponies: he asks 110 per cent of them but never goes over the top and breaks them. There is never any blood in the mouth of a pony Paul has played.

Every year, once the Gold Cup is over, Withers takes Cowdray ponies to Deauville, for the Lancel Gold Cup tournament. In 1991, playing Back for Tacones Farm, he helped his team to a 10-5 win over Chateau Giscours in the final of the Jaeger Lecoultre Cup, but without Archie.

Archie doesn't go to Deauville any more. The racing on the track around the polo ground absolutely mesmerised him and he forgot all about polo.

A pony remembered for different reasons is Gretchen. At the age of 13, Michael Pearson, Lord Cowdray's elder son, was put up on Gretchen, 'who was uncontrollable, nobody else wanted to ride her'.

I found myself on Cowdray Golf Course and Gretchen decided to take off. She was completely out of control as we came towards a bunker with a deer fence on the other side. I thought she wouldn't possibly be able to stop: she did, and I didn't, and I ended up in the bunker with concussion. After that, various people tried to get me to take up polo, including Sinclair Hill, who actually managed to get me wielding a polo stick, but my riding days were over . . .

Although Michael Pearson has left the active part in polo to his younger brother, Charles, he is nevertheless devoted to the game and to the club.

The Hon. Michael Pearson and his wife, Marina

I never played, but I can remember being taken down to the Lawns as a child at weekends, and to watch a game was great excitement. It was a wonderful afternoon for us, as children. One of my early memories - I suppose I was about seven - was of the Queen and Prince Philip coming to lunch at the house before a match. We children had been practising with Nanny in the nursery as to how to address them - I know I had to bow and say 'Good morning, Your Majesty'. And, in those days, we had cocktail parties every weekend at the house: everyone would come, and most of them ended up in the swimming pool afterwards. . .

Will Lucas, at a handicap of 6, is another of the leading UK players from Cowdray Park. The grandson of Arthur Lucas, the Woolmers Park patron, he also began polo at Pony Club level, although he remembers watching polo 'at the age of one or two with a little stick in my hand'. Nearly thirty years later, Will - and his brother, James - is a familiar figure on English polo grounds, of which Cowdray remains his favourite, as with most people because of the unchanging atmosphere.

The first tournament I ever won at Cowdray was the Park House - I must have been about 15 at the time - but in those days I only played during the school holidays with my father, John, who had been one of the best players in England, with a 6 handicap at the height of his career. I left school and the Pony Club at the same time and spent four years working with a commercial property company in London. I never regretted those years in London - it was very much the 'boom' time - but I suddenly realised at the age of twenty-two that I would regret for life not knowing how good I could have been at polo.

In 1987, the year Lucas escaped from London, he was chosen to play in the Cartier International at Guards, together with Howard and Julian Hipwood and Alan Kent: 'I think I broke the mould for the first time in fifteen years!' His favourite pony at the time was Matilda, a liver chestnut from the Argentine which he had ridden from the time she was twelve - in 1987 she was about seventeen.

My mother told me that Matilda was too old for the International, but said I could ride her in the pre-match procession, which I knew Matilda would love. But I had every intention of giving her the second chukka, as well. Unknown to me, Mother read my thoughts and during the first chukka went to the pony lines, ordered Matilda to be untacked and the tack locked up! Matilda knew what was happening: she turned her back on the game and sulked for the rest of the match . . . She had already been in the Gold Cup final in Deauville and I went on playing her until she was about twenty.

Will Lucas has won every low and medium goal tournament in which he has played. In 1990 he was picked for John Horswell's team, Sladmore, then the only non-professional team in the UK; and was with them again in 1991 when they were the only all-English side.

In the winter of 1987, Lucas went to the Argentine, to stay with Jorge

Will Lucas has won every low and medium goal tournament in which he has played. He is seen (below), left, in action for Broncos against Frasers

ing there.

If you want to play the best polo - and not be paid for it - you have to go to the Argentine. I was always brought up to believe in polo as a sport in the old term, and I won't play with someone I don't like. I know that, often, I have not been picked for a team because of my attitude, but I value my independence and I refuse to drop my standards.

In his Pony Club days Will Lucas won the Handley Cross match, together with three members of the Dukes family, Sarah and 'the twins', Jeremy and Sean. With their brother Paul (2), the 1-handicapped twins (so identical that even close friends find it difficult to tell them apart) played for a time in a family team, Drumco. Their sister Sarah, polo correspondent for *The Independent* and herself an occasional player with a -1 handicap, remembers the help given to her brothers by Lucas.

Polo wasn't on the curriculum in our Pony Club, so we played with Will at Cowdray. Sean really took up the game again at Cambridge, and has never looked back!

Sarah was largely responsible for encouraging Tim Fane, today a rising star on the Cowdray scene, to take up the game. Twenty-eight-year old Fane, who runs his own yard at Blackdown House, in the rolling Hampshire countryside near Winchester, has enjoyed a meteoric career, especially as he rode a horse for the first time only four years ago.

My ambition was to be a mechanical engineer. When I qualified I discovered the salary I was offered was less than I considered I was worth. It was about this time that Paul Dukes, after a good deal of badgering, persuaded me to sit on a horse. I progressed to a very quiet polo pony, found that I didn't fall off too often and started to enjoy the game. I decided to buy a pony of my own; Will Lucas sold me one - then the rot set in!

Stick and pen: Tim Fane and Sarah Dukes

Fane played for two seasons at Tidworth, with two ponies, acquiring a 0 handicap. Two more ponies were added to his stables but with playing membership of the major clubs closed he began to feel frustrated.

How could I get in? Then I had a brainwave: I would hire a professional to play with me on a one season basis. Alex Parrott, the New Zealand player, was desperate to come over here, so we hired ourselves to Tony Nagle at the Royal Berkshire, who had also taken Will Lucas into his team, Corsair.

The 1990 season was a highly successful one for the team, and Tim Fane's handicap rose to 2. Alex Parrott (now a 4-goaler) joined the new Knepp Castle team, Knepptunes, winners of the 1991 Dollar Cup at Cowdray Park, while Fane, now full of confidence, went to play medium goal with John Seabrook's Lambourn team and low goal with Richard Guess's Cowdray-based Rowleys. His handicap rose to 3 in mid-season.

I had always enjoyed watching polo at Cowdray and at the end of the 1990 season I applied for chukka membership. I was turned down and then, a month later, Tidworth announced it was closing the membership which left me, having won cup after cup with a 2 handicap and few horses, with nowhere to play.

Fane wrote again to Cowdray Park, pointing out his dilemma. This time he was accepted for chukka membership.

I shall always be grateful to Cowdray Park. I had started to feel out on a limb, especially as my handicap remained at 3 when the HPA decided to lower the handicap of much better, and more experienced, English players. I'm only a goal less than Nicky Evans, who has been playing far longer than me. Paul Dukes,who is infinitely more experienced, is now a goal less than me, a newcomer! This season, I've felt more under pressure: people expect you to do something different as a 3-goaler. My riding is not too bad - perhaps I was born with the knack - and I certainly took to it like the proverbial duck to water. However, I am not convinced that my hitting is as good as it should be, although if I can get a handicap of 3 in so short a time, anything must be possible!

Like many other young players, Tim Fane was off to the Argentine last winter - 'it might help me to play to my handicap in 1992' he said modestly, shortly before his departure. Spectators at Cowdray Park will see

Following the game. Above: Midhurst-based 5-handicap player Martin 'Sticky' Glue (left) and Peter Pattenden, patron of People Skills International. Below: The first photograph taken at Cowdray Park of the then Lady Diana Spencer, July, 1980

more of Tim in the future, and he insists that he is in the club's debt.

If I had not been accepted as a chukka member I would definitely have given up the game - I was frustrated with nowhere to go. Because of Cowdray Park I have had a fantastic season.

Force Ten will be remembered by many spectators and players at Cowdray Park as the name of a pony and of a successful team. The pony, still covering at Peter Grace's stud, near Ascot, was the favourite mount of Peter Gilbert who, in the late 1970s, formed a team with Antonio Herrera, Patrick Churchward and Phil Rhodes.

Peter Gilbert, who now runs the Pinhooker Stud, near Petworth, had played in India, from where many of his ponies came, and in Dubai, where

Treading in: C. S. Brooks patron Brook Johnson and Mrs Kerry Packer

he founded the Dubai Polo Club. Equally well-remembered at Cowdray will be Gilbert's pointer, Bramble, now a gallant old lady of fifteen.

Like David Jamison, Peter Gilbert is endeavouring to recreate country house polo. He has laid out a three-quarter size polo ground at Pinhooker (the name comes from someone who buys yearlings and sells them on as two-year-olds); but he is still very much a non-playing member at Cowdray Park.

CHUKKA SIX

A Season at Cowdray Park

The Ball no Question makes of Ayes and Noes, But Here or There, as strikes the Player, goes; And He that toss'd you down into the Field, He knows about it all, He knows, HE knows! *(Rubaiyat of Omar Khayyam)*

It rained at Ambersham on Sunday for the first medium goal league game to have been played at Cowdray Park for some time. However, like the swallows who ignored the weather to offer a foretaste of approaching summer, the home team was undaunted by the elements or by the apparent invincibility of Rowleys. Omar Sosa (9), who has a different handicap for different countries, appeared to set the pace in the first chukka. A fourth goal in the first few seconds of the second chukka seemed to confirm his devastating ability to unsettle Cowdray Park. Then, Charles Fraser (2) scored a goal from Chris Bethell (4) and another from a long shot by Paul Withers (7). A penalty shot by Withers brought the score to 3-4 at the end of the second. In the third, Sosa put Rowleys three goals ahead; but Cowdray had the bit between its teeth, and good shots by Withers and Bethell saw the chukka end 5-6. There was only one point between the teams when the penultimate chukka ended; and in the fifth Withers exhibited all his old skill to give Cowdray Park a most satisfactory victory, 9-7.

Our first match report of the 1991 season boded well for Cowdray Park, although not for spectators if the weather forecast was to be believed. As it happened, last year was one of the wettest on record at Cowdray for the first three months, although it did little to dampen the enthusiasm of members. The Raj Mata of Jaipur remembers the spectators as 'great followers of the game' and, today, Charles Fraser notes the partisanship at Cowdray, even in wet weather.

We have a very dedicated crowd following, even at the beginning of the season. They know everyone playing, even the names of the ponies.

That first report of the year covered the opening match of the Texaco League, the league format having been introduced at domestic level in

The first final of the 1991 season saw Broncos win the Tyro Cup, 10-7½, in a match against Panthers. With Rosemary Harper, who made the presentation, are (from left) Will Lucas, Guy Farley, Tomas Ezcurra and the Marquess of Milford Haven

order to give members a better share of match play. To this end, the Farewell Cup, traditionally the last of the season, and the new Autumn Cup lengthened the season by two weeks in September. In the end, the Texaco Trophy was won on 19th May by the pink-shirted Panthers, Mark Franklin's team, who, having received a half handicap, beat People Skills International 10½-5. A match report is again appropriate:

Panthers went straight into the attack with a goal by Charles Seavill (4) and never looked back. Will Roberts (3) was the epitome of a polo player, scoring twice in the first chukka, and Panthers ensured their lead with a beautiful under the neck

Ian Gould of Panthers with his groom, Clare Hood

shot by Ian Gould (5), an Australian who played last year for Kerry Packer. Stuart Mackenzie (8) kept PSI in the game in the third and fourth chukkas but the Texaco Trophy was already well and truly in Panthers' sights. Ian Gould's pony, Correntina, was declared Best Turned Out (groom, Clare Hood) and the Best Young Player was Stuart Dickson (0) of PSI . . .

Polo began at Cowdray Park last season on Saturday, 27th April, with the quarter finals of the medium-goal Tyro Cup, that pre-war Roehampton trophy, in weather noted as 'dull'. Indeed, until the end of June, the weather was reported consistently as 'wet', 'damp', 'cold' or 'freezing', and the first notice to be headed 'hot' appeared for 29th June for the final of the Midhurst Town Cup.

A good partnership was formed by Charles Seavill and the 2-handicap Panthers patron, Mark Franklin, in the final on 6th May against Guy Farley's Broncos. Will Lucas, the 6-goaler grandson of the late Woolmers Park patron Arthur Lucas, and Tomas Ezcurra, usually the steady 6-goaler for Cowdray Park, gradually narrowed the score. At the end of the day it was Ezcurra who surged ahead to win the Tyro for Broncos, 10-7½.

A cold day on 18th May saw Trend (received ½) beat Rowleys, 10½-8, in the final of the Jersey Lilies Cup, a match which combined youth and experience to a fine degree. Trend included Alice Harvey (-1), a young Pony Club star, and Adam Buchanan (2), another youngster usually playing for Tramontana, who proved himself man of the match. Third place for Trend was taken by Anthony Embiricos (3), player-patron of Tramontana who, later in the season, was to play in his team's fifth Gold Cup win since 1986.

Many players, of course, had not stopped playing since the last season, moving on from Cowdray to France, then to South America or Australia. At Cowdray Park, however, the home team's ponies are generally brought in from pasture by the middle of February, as Jackie Wright explains:

We bring them in then so that they can have six weeks roadwork before practice begins, rather like hunters. Stick and balling begins at the end of March, for a month, usually on the House Ground with chukkas on Saturday and Sunday mornings. We are usually the first British club to start because the House Ground drains so well compared with grounds at other clubs.

It should be emphasised, perhaps, that ponies are not simply turned out for the winter months: they are checked at least twice a day. But throughout the autumn and winter the sight of some of the finest animals in the world becomes familiar to motorists and walkers in Cowdray Park or, today, in Harting Combe, near Rogate, where Kerry Packer's string earns a well-deserved rest.

The 1991 season also began with interesting developments at Stedham, Packer's grounds some three miles up-river from Cowdray Park. Played for the first time in 1990, the following season was to see them used more frequently in the run-up to the Gold Cup; and they proved invaluable during the intensive period of wet weather, relieving the Ambersham grounds, themselves in constant use to protect the grounds at the River and Lawns. Despite some opposition from Stedham people - due mainly to controversy over a previously little-used footpath - Kerry Packer received conditional planning permission, for an initial three-year period, to use the land for polo.

It is usually fatal to predict winners in the various cups at Cowdray. But from early in the 1991 season, Tramontana appeared on a winning streak. On 26th May, another cold day, a team comprising Embiricos, Antonio Herrera, the Mexican maestro Carlos Gracida and young Buchanan won the high-goal Smith Ryland Cup, beating the holders, Cowdray Park 9-7. The home team, with Charles Pearson at No. 1, Alan Kent at No. 3 and Paul Withers at Back, had an interesting substitute for Tomas Ezcurra: the 6-handicap Lord Charles Beresford, a scion of the Waterford polo dynasty. As we noted at the time:

Despite a magnificent effort, Cowdray were no match in the end for the power of the Mexicans, Gracida and Herrera. Gracida converted a penalty, Herrera put Tramontana ahead after a struggle and, with seconds left, Gracida made the deciding shot. Nevertheless, if Cowdray retain this high-goal team for the season all will not be lost . . .

Beresford did not play for Cowdray again that season and, as those utterly impartial gods watching over polo decided, Tramontana were to be the high-goal side of 1991.

The futility of predicting winners was apparent on 19th May, a dull afternoon at Ambersham, when Polo Plus beat Frasers 9-8 in the final of the Cicero Cup, a medium-goal tournament. The presence at No. 3 in the Frasers line-up of 8-goaler Julian Hipwood surely boded well for his team; but after equalising in the fourth chukka, Hipwood suffered his second fall of the weekend - the first came the previous day while he was playing for Guardacre in a Queen's Cup league match. Frasers appeared to throw away chance after chance as a result, although Polo Plus were probably surprised to find themselves winning by only one goal.

Polo Plus, winners of the 1991 Cicero Cup. From left: Adrian Wade, Garth Bearman. Andrew Seavill, Jonathan Wade

The first match of June saw the River Ground used for a final for the first time last season. Crawley Park (received $1^1/_2$) lost 8-$5^1/_2$ to Les Lions in the Robert Fraser Cup, a trophy presented by the sponsors of the Polo Plus opponents. The medium-goal match began in tedious fashion, but the game livened up after Will Scherer, the 5-handicap No. 3 for Les Lions, lived up to his reputation and scored twice in the second chukka.

If anything, the match proved that little can be read into a team receiving a goal, or even a half, on handicap. An example, much later in the season, was offered in a qualifying match for the medium-goal Harrison Cup, played between Ellerston White and Mill Farm (received $^1/_2$) at

Ambersham. The Ellerston line-up was Alastair Archibald (2), Jim Gilmore (5), Alan Kent (7) and Matt MacKenzie-Hill (2).

Ellerston romped away from the start (we noted in the match report) and one is tempted to say that had this team played on Sunday (21st July, Gold Cup Day) Ellerston would have taken the Gold Cup to Australia. Despite the presence of Hector Galindo (8) in Mill Farm his side simply did not have the necessary power - several shots ended just before the goal mouth, for instance. nevertheless, it was a good display of medium-goal polo, played in perfect (if uncommon) weather . . .

Jim Gilmore of Ellerston

A final on the Lawns - a mild and breezy occasion - on 2nd June saw Richard Guess's Rowleys win the *Country Life* sponsored Duke of Sutherland Cup. The cup, first won in June 1953 by the 'robin egg blue' American team, Meadow Brook, who beat Cowdray Park 6-5*, is a treasured trophy at Cowdray and, last season, gave spectators a chance to see a new overseas team, Royal Pahang, captained by HRH Tenku Mahkota, heir to the throne of one of the Malaysian Federation states. The diminutive prince, inherently courteous, added a new dimension to partisanship at Cowdray Park by travelling with a band of vociferous supporters.

It was a 10-7 victory for Rowleys, with superb teamwork, especially

*'Presentation of the Cup and dispersal of spectators delayed the start of the following game' is the unusual entry in the scorebook for 3rd June, 1956, when Cowdray Park won the Duke of Sutherland Cup, 8-2½, in a match against Windsor Park. The delayed match, a league game, saw Cowdray again victorious: beating Fred Withers's Whip Hill 7-4½ in four chukkas.

by high-goalers Omar Sosa (9) and Hector Galindo (8).

The same day saw the final of the Dollar Cup, with victory for the newest team in West Sussex, Kim Richardson's Knepptunes, based on the Knepp Castle estate, east of Cowdray near Shipley. Knepptunes very much reflect the early days of Cowdray Park - friendly matches on fields in the middle of quiet countryside and (perhaps the only difference) the local pub as a club house. Certainly their success saw that the Dollar Cup, commemorating Peter Dollar, a notable player post-war at Cowdray, remained in the county. Their opponents, Hotel Design, lost 8-3, despite the presence, at No. 2, of the Earl of Tyrone, brother of Charles Beresford.

The rise of clubs such as Knepptunes, and the grounds at Stedham, Westerlands and elsewhere in the district, is due in no small measure to the existence of Cowdray Park. The prophecy, made in 1919 by *Polo Monthly*, that Cowdray could become the centre for a group of southern tournaments, appears in many ways to be fulfilled, as Richard Guess notes:

As one gets older, it is better to keep physically fit by playing as much as possible - it doesn't matter what your sport might be. The satellite clubs have grown out of people's desire to play polo, and they all compliment Cowdray Park club. We all love playing polo, and we all love Cowdray Park: the more satellite clubs there are, the better.

The greatly increased play during the last two seasons, and the continuation of stick and ball and friendly games during the winter months on Terry Hanlon's fields at Ambersham, is another fulfilment, albeit unintentional, of an Edwardian ambition. In 1908, two years before Harold Cowdray set up his Capron House team, the West Sussex Polo Club had come into being at Pulborough, east of Midhurst*. It was short lived, although it achieved membership of the Hurlingham Polo Association in its second season; but as the secretary, G.H. Johnstone of Bignor Park, remarked at the time, 'Our aim is to play as early as we like and without cessation to the early days of October.'

On 9th June history was made at Cowdray Park. The high-goal Cooch Behar Cup was postponed because of rain and the final of the low-

*The grounds were on the Stopham estate, owned by the Bartelott family for six centuries. The president of the club was Earl Winterton, from Shillinglee Park, beyond Petworth. A distinguished horseman, but no polo player, Winterton, who died in 1962, was for nearly half a century MP for Horsham and was known as the Father of the House of Commons, his Irish peerage enabling him to sit there.

Gonzalo Pieres

Ellerston patron Kerry Packer (right) with Ian Gould

goal Barrett Cup was played for the first time on the House Ground. Richard Guess's Rowleys defeated Panthers 6-5 in four chukkas, with Tim Fane, playing at No. 2 for Rowleys, proving himself man of the match.

A week later, Kerry Packer's 'A' team, Ellerston White, had an equally narrow victory, 13-12, over Santa Fe in the final of the Argentine Ambassador's Cup, a trophy presented first in 1961. Played as part of the Cirencester-based Warwickshire Cup league, it was the first trophy won by the Whites in the 1991 season and, despite torrential rain, the crowd turned up in force to see a magnificent display of polo. As usual, the 10-goal Pieres brothers, Alfonso and Gonzalo, played as one, although their cousin, 'Juni' Crotto, the 9 handicap No. 3 for Santa Fe, gave them a run for their money until half time.

The strength of a team such as Ellerston White, and its sister team Ellerston Black, lies obviously in the purchasing power of the sponsor or patron, and there is no doubt that since his arrival on the Cowdray Park scene, Kerry Packer has been a considerable influence on high-goal polo. Unlike many teams he was able to fall back on fresh, unplayed, ponies once the Gold Cup was over, and he proved generous in lending mounts to other teams. The reverse side of the coin, however, reflects the feeling of many low- or medium-handicapped players that the ability of one or two patrons to pay for high-goal Argentinian players - the 'hired assasins' as they have been termed - has a deleterious effect on sportsmanship. David Jamison, for example, prefers to play his high-goal polo in America; and while Charles Pearson feels that it is unrealistic to expect a certain standard of polo without highly-paid professionals, the face of high-goal polo at Cowdray Park, and elsewhere in England, has altered dramatically since the arrival of the South American professionals over the last twenty years.

Conversely, during the Falklands War and its aftermath, initial panic at Cowdray Park about the blockade on new ponies and high-goal players proved unfounded, as Charles Pearson recalls:

The Argentine invasion of the Falklands in 1982 took place the weekend before chukkas started. Immediately everyone said that there would be no high-goal polo. But an extraordinary resourcefullness came out of it, even though the outbreak of hostilities between two polo-playing nations could not have come at a worse time. Within hours telephone lines around the world were buzzing and not a single team dropped out of the Gold Cup. No-one began to import ponies from the Argentine again until the trade ban was lifted about 1986, but there was no shortage of ponies. In a way, the war did a great deal of good for English polo: it made us realise that we could run high-goal tournaments without the Argentinians.

The postponed Cooch Behar Cup final was played on 16th June, between the 1990 winners, Cowdray Park, and the Ambersham-based

The Raj Mata of Jaipur presents the Cooch Behar Cup to Ambersham-based C.S. Brooks

American team, C.S. Brooks, who won 6-5 after an extra chukka. An equalising goal in the third chukka made the outcome unpredictable, and Thomas Ezcurra, Cowdray's No. 2 equalised again at the end of what should have been the last chukka. The Raj Mata of Jaipur, sister of the donor of the trophy, made the presentation to a team that certainly caught the imagination of spectators during the 1991 season; and the fact that Tim Johnson, brother of C.S. Brooks patron, Brook Johnson, is to run a low-goal team for 1992 provides a bonus for followers of the white-shirted players.

Extra time was needed, too, for the final of the Midhurst Town Cup on 29th June, when Tramontana beat Cowdray Park 10-9. The cup, presented first in the post-war revival days, is very much a symbol of Midhurst Chamber of Trade's gratitude to Cowdray Park Polo Club. As Johnnie Kidd emphasises:

Polo at Cowdray Park rubs off on the town. How successful would some of the businesses be without polo? It is a local industry and I would reckon that, because of polo, up to £1 million is spent in the area each season.

Another match report is worth repeating:

Tramontana won the Midhurst Town Cup in an exciting match against the home team. Alan Kent was man of the match for Cowdray Park, putting his team ahead in the third chukka. Tramontana, four times winners of the Cowdray Park Gold Cup, fought back brilliantly and the star of the side was undoubtedly Adolfo Cambiaso who, although only just 16 years of

Cambiaso: 'boy wonder' of the 1991 season

age, has a handicap of 7. At the end of the sixth chukka, Cowdray captain Paul Withers equalised, 9-9, which meant the game went into extra time for a sudden death goal. The near-legendary Mexican player, Carlos Gracida (10), scored the deciding goal for Tramontana.

Later the same afternoon the final of the Benson Cup, presented after the war by Sir Rex Benson, was something of an anti-climax. Red Cell, including Chris Bethell and David Morley, beat Marabunta 4-3 in this low-goal match, the game having gone into extra time twice. The weather was hot, although Ambersham was still being used, standing up well to the extra play. And it was at Ambersham, on 10th July, that one of the invitation matches, for which Cowdray Park is so famous, made a refreshing break from the intensity of the British Open Championship for the Gold Cup, which had started eight days earlier.

The invitation match was between a low-goal Cowdray Park team and four players from Zimbabwe*. As we noted at the time, 'Young Cowdray' upheld the traditions of the club, putting themselves firmly in the lead in the first chukka. Although Zimbabwe lost, 2-7, a refreshing aspect was that all the goals were field goals, not the result of penalty shots.

Two days later crowds flocked to the Lawns for the second annual charity match in aid of King Edward VII Hospital, Midhurst. Formally opened by Edward VII eighty-five years earlier, the hospital, originally a sanatorium for tuberculosis sufferers, is today internationally-known for its work with chest diseases, hip replacement surgery, coronary heart disease, orthopaedics and many other conditions. The match, which formed part of the British Open, was sponsored by People Skills International, Peter Pattenden's management development and sales training organisation, which has its own team, medium-goal players including Terry Hanlon, the Cowdray Park commentator and coach, and Mike Rutherford of the 'pop' group, Genesis.

In 1990, over £30,000 was raised for the hospital, although there was disappointment when the Prince of Wales retired from the Windsor Park team following his accident at Cirencester. Last year, however, the Prince was in fighting form as Back for his team, although they lost 8-11 to a high-goal Cowdray Park side.

Windsor Park	Cowdray Park
1. Geoffrey Kent (3)	1. Hon Charles Pearson (2)
2. Rod Matthews (5)	2. Tomas Ezcurra (6)
3. Pite Merlos (10)	3. Alan Kent (7)
Bk. HRH The Prince of Wales (4)	Bk. Paul Withers (7)

The game was tinged with sadness when, shortly after Merlos had equalised in the first chukka, Withers's 12-year-old pony Cacique, col-

*Cowdray Park: 1. H. Brett (0), 2. C. Seavill (4), 3. R. Graham (5), Bk. Jack Kidd (2); Zimbabwe: 1. A. Greenshields (2), 2. E. Meikle (4), 3. P. Kuhn (3), Bk. K. Taylor (2).

Above: The Prince of Wales in action. Below: Cowdray Park, winners of the 1991 PSI Trophy, with Lord Cowdray and Mrs Peter Pattenden, wife of the PSI patron. From Left: Charles Pearson, Tomas Ezcurra, Alan Kent and captain Paul Withers

lapsed and died from a heart attack. The Press, whose presence was inevitable on such an occasion, were remarkably restrained under the circumstances, even *The Sun* inserting only a brief report, hidden away on an inside page, about the Prince 'comforting a polo pal' whose pony had died.

In the fourth chukka, which started with the teams equal, Withers put Cowdray ahead and, despite good work from Merlos, Cowdray Park was unbeatable. Sadly, the match saw too many penalties awarded and, as we noted at the time, the umpires seemed uncertain of the elementary rules of the game.

On 19th July, Anthony Embiricos's Tramontana booked their place in the Gold Cup final, beating Kerry Packer's Ellerston Black 17-5 on the Black's home ground at Stedham. Earlier, it had seemed that the final would be played out between the two Ellerston teams, but the combined power of Carlos Gracida and the 'boy-wonder' Adolfo Cambiaso, who had recently celebrated his sixteenth birthday, took the four times winners back into the Open. Even then, it was obvious that Cambiaso, shortly to go from 7 to 9, would join the Ellerston squad for the 1992 season.

The weekend of 20th-21st July saw the ultimate in high-goal polo at Cowdray Park: the Gold Cup final. A brilliantly hot Saturday at the House Grounds was the setting for the twenty-eighth Park House Cup final, with Bears (received $^1/_2$) beating Giraffes $5^1/_2$-2. Another youngster, 17-year-old Henry Brett, who first played with the Kirtlington Pony Club, set the pace for the winners, playing to perfection in a game that, not only because of its setting, recalled to many older spectators the early post-war years at Cowdray.

Ione O'Brien and Henry Brett

The River Ground may be the favourite field for most players, but on a warm summer day there is little to beat the

House Ground, with its views of Charlton Forest and the South Downs. The Downs were immortalised by G.K. Chesterton as symbolising the best of English quality because 'those colossal contours . . . are at the same time soft and strong.' Unintentionally, he summarised polo at Cowdray Park at the same time.

The Saturday also saw the finals of the high-goal Jack Gannon Trophy, a scrappy game in which Alfa Romeo beat John Horswell's all-English team, Sladmore, 7-5; and the Tatham Cup, commemorating polo manager 'Bolshie' Tatham, in which Guardacre beat Los Locos 11-10 after an extra chukka.

The following day saw the Raj Mata of Jaipur on duty to present the Gold Cup to Tramontana, and here another match report must be permitted.

Tramontana regained the Gold Cup after a two year interval at the Lawns on Sunday. A record crowd of between 6,000 and 7,000 saw an exciting match between two splendidly matched teams, although from the second chukka the combination of Carlos Gracida (10) and Adolfo Cambiaso (7) was to prove irresistible, even to the combined 20-goal power of the Pieres brothers, playing at No. 2 and No. 3 for Ellerston White. There were too many goals from penalties in the first half and, in the second, Ellerston tended to panic. By the end of the fourth, there was little doubt about the outcome and while Gonzalo Pieres scored twice for Ellerston in quick succession, Gracida and Cambiaso had the edge on all their opponents. Tramontana patron Anthony Embiricos (2) proved that he is worthy of a higher handicap, particularly with a brilliant pass to Gracida in the fifth. The score for Tramontana could have been higher - the sixth saw Cambiaso up to goal unopposed (as is often the case when he plays) but his stick broke as he prepared to take his final shot.

The subsidiary Ashton Cup was won by C.S. Brooks, who defeated Santa Fe 12-6. Originally a Hurlingham trophy, the Ashton had been widely seen as going to the red-shirted Santa Fe but despite hard riding by Heracio Heguy (10) - like the Pieres brothers, a member of a South American polo dynasty - his team never entered into the feeling of the match. The power of US captain Owen Rinehart, playing for Brooks as No. 3, and his No. 1 team-mate, Tim Stakemire (3), put the Whites ahead by four in the first half and, from then, Santa Fe appeared to rely, unfairly, on Heguy for any goals. The delight of the winners, who throughout the season had lost one game at Cowdray Park, was obvious and infectious.

Above: Tramontana and Ellerston White line up for the 1991 Gold Cup final.
Below: C.S. Brooks, winners of the subsidiary Ashton Cup

A week after the Gold Cup four familiar Cowdray faces, Will and James Lucas, Julian Hipwood and Alan Kent, made up the England team to face New Zealand in the Cartier International Coronation Cup match at Guards Polo Club. It was the coming-of-age of International Day, and the eighth to be sponsored by Cartier; and while a proportion of profits go to provide scholarships and grants for young English players to play overseas in the winter, and make a welcome addition to HPA funds, the atmosphere at Smith's Lawn is far removed from the friendliness of Cowdray Park. The crowds who came to Cowdray to see the Coronation Cup in 1953 may have contributed towards a record attendance, but they came to see polo which, sadly, cannot be said for the crowds who filled the stands and enclosures at Guards. Of course, it was an enjoyable outing, the weather was far removed from the average summer's day and the picnics outdid each other in splendour, Yet, at the end of the day, regular Cowdray Park spectators who had travelled up from Sussex to support the England team missed the familiar, homely, setting of Ambersham or the Lawns or the River Ground. The glitz of International Day at Guards is not for those happy with a car rug or a cushion on the stand at Cowdray.

Half-time: James Lucas (left) and Charles Fraser

The result of the match, 12-10 in favour of New Zealand, was disappointing for Julian Hipwood, coming to the end of his two decades as England captain. While England was two points ahead at half-time, due largely to a hat-trick from Alan Kent in the first chukka, New Zealand equalised in the fourth and went ahead by one goal in the fifth. Alan Kent equalised in the final chukka, but Andrew Parrott, playing at Back for New Zealand scored the deciding goal in the last few seconds.

Hipwood had taken the place of the 5-goal Andrew Seavill who, later in the day, played in an HPA team which lost 6-7½ to the Prince of Wales's Team in the Jubilee Cup. Seavill is, at twenty-six, the youngest of three polo-playing brothers - the others are 30-years-old Charles and Hector, who is twenty-nine - who have been devoted to Cowdray Park since they played there first in 1985.

One of the most attractive things about Cowdray Park is still the atmosphere (says their father, Colin Seavill, who began to play polo at the Rutland Club twenty years ago). We much prefer it to the glitter of Guards or the Royal Berkshire, although that is not to say that there is no good polo at those clubs.

The Seavill brothers grew up in Lincolnshire, where their father attempted to introduce an alternative sport to hunting - 'and to encourage people to play polo, rather than simply watch their crops grow in the summer months'. The result was a highly successful team, Cream Gorse, named after a famous covert in the Quorn country, where the boys had all ridden in Pony Club days.

Our best season was in 1980, when we won the Dollar Cup at Cowdray Park (recalls Colin Seavill). As I faded out and Charles took my place, we realised that Rutland could not offer anything as challenging as Cowdray Park where polo was concerned; so Cowdray Park it had to be!

The Seavills are based today at Trotton, a stone's throw from Midhurst, and Charles in particular has made an impression on spectators with his teamwork in Panthers, Mark Franklin's pink-shirted squad.

'There is never a loser in polo - someone always comes second,' as Cowdray Park commentator Terry Hanlon always declares through his

En famille: Charles Seavill (standing) with, from left, Andrew, Colin and Hector

microphone. Ellerston White, having played well, but unsuccessfully, in the Gold Cup final were to carry off two trophies from Cowdray in what has become very much a distinct second season of polo. On 3rd August, they beat Palmera 7-$6\frac{1}{2}$ in the final of the medium-goal Harrison Cup and, the following day, won the Holden White Cup, beating Las Estrellas $5\frac{1}{2}$-3. Playing in perfect polo weather on the Lawns, the second match saw Ellerston's manager, the 5-handicap Jim Gilmore, giving his final performance of the 1992 season at Cowdray Park - and more than living up to his reputation as a demonic rider and vocally demonstrative player.

The last day of the old Glorious Goodwood Week, known now as the Festival Meeting, saw a belated summer arrive at Cowdray: perfect polo weather at last. At Ambersham, two medium-goal finals resulted in

Panthers won the 1991 Aotea Cup by a $\frac{1}{2}$ handicap. From left: Ian Gould, Charles Seavill, Mrs Stuart Mackenzie, Lord Cowdray, patron Mark Franklin, Will Roberts

Panthers beating Les Lions $4\frac{1}{2}$-4 in the Aotea and Whitehall, based at the Cheshire Polo Club, carrying off the Maidensgrove Cup after an $8\frac{1}{2}$-4 victory over Stilemans.

The last high-goal match of the season, the final of the Cowdray Park Challenge Cup on 4th August, resulted in one of the best scores of the year: Los Locos, with Will Lucas's aunt Clare Tomlinson at No. 1, beat Windsor Park 15-8. From the start, Locos were firmly in the lead, with No. 3 Mike

Arauco (7) scoring twice, albeit from penalties, and Simon Tomlinson, husband of Clare, taking the score to 6-2 with a superb drive into goal.

There was a bonus for Los Locos. Clare Tomlinson's pony, Ludvika, ridden by the 7-handicap Martin Vidou, received the Vickers Cup for the best heavyweight; while Roberta, ridden by Pite Merlos, No. 3 for Windsor Park, won the Brooke Joynson Cup for the best lightweight in the game.

The most exciting final of the first weekend in August was for the Ruins Cup, with Bulldogs beating Frasers 4-3 in a fifth, and extra, chukka. Frasers, the 8-goal team raised by Colin Emson of merchant bankers Robert Fraser Partners, had won the low-goal trophy the previous season - and failed now by a hair's breadth to retain it. Robert Hanson (1), playing at No. 2 for Bulldogs, equalised in the fourth chukka, and a good attempt by Emson (1), Frasers' Back, to score the winning goal was spoiled when the ball missed by inches.

Ludvika (left) and Roberta: prizewinners in the Cowdray Park Challenge Cup final

The final saw good play by another youngster, hopefully to remain on the polo circuit in the future: 14-year-old Satnam Dhillon, after whom a proud father has named his Cirencester-based team.

From 9th to 11th August the Pony Club National Championships, sponsored by the *Daily Telegraph,* culminated in the finals at Ambersham. The Pony Club polo season begins in early July each year, with the first of twelve major tournaments held across the country starting at Epsom. Some two hundred players, making up fifty-two teams, came to Cowdray Park, with four groups competing for their own championship, youngsters under the age of fourteen; under-sixteens, under-nineteens and the, most senior, under-21s. Generally, Pony Club polo is thriving, as John Wright, who heads the voluntary committee, explained:

Eleven new branches joined the fraternity last year (1990) and in 1991 we welcomed new teams from seven branches. Each new branch enjoys the generous support of the Hurlingham Polo Association, the governing body, and the Whitbread Trust, who between them provide a starter pack of £250 worth of sticks, short hand sticks and balls to every new branch. A total of 102 young players were to benefit from places on four high-grade courses, as against seventy-two in 1990. In addition, David Jamison is running a pilot Fast Track Scheme for six 14 to 18-year-olds with outstanding potential. . .

The establishment of Cowdray Park as a permanent annual venue for the championships has proved of enormous benefit to Pony Club members, many of whom will doubtless follow in the footsteps of their predecessors, Nicky Evans, Will Lucas and Oliver Ellis. Indeed, Satnam Dhillon and Henry Brett are helping to continue a healthy tradition.

The 1991 final was an especially memorable occasion for Cowdray Park: Cowdray Pony Club won the Daily Telegraph Trophy for the under-21s, with a 5-3½ win over the Royal Artillery. It was not a predestined victory: Cowdray were in poor form for the early part of the four-chukka game, with Eddie Hobden (1), playing at No. 2, scoring their only goal before half-time, which ended 3½-1 in favour of the RA. Jack Kidd, son of Johnnie, playing off a 2-handicap, made a run down worthy of his father for a sixty-yard penalty shot, but hit the ball inches wide. It was Hobden who eventually narrowed the RA lead to their received half, and Cowdray came to life. As we reported:

Alexander Baillieu (1) scored from Henry Brett (0) in a melee and then Brett, who has shown so much sparkle this season, sent the ball up to Kidd to see victory at 5 3½.

Eddie Hobden was named the Daily Telegraph Best Player of the Match, another laurel to the home team, whose seniors had not enjoyed their best season.

In the Rendell Cup, a two-chukka final for under-19s, an equaliser at the very end of the second resulted in one of the famous Pony Club 'run downs' between clubs from the Hampshire Hunt and the Quorn. Both sides took a ball down the ground, the first over the line - in this case the Quorn - being the winner.

Cowdray Park Pony Club, winners of the Daily Telegraph Trophy

It was appropriate, perhaps, that this exhilarating day saw the introduction of another Pony Club trophy: the Young Telegraph Award for the Most Promising Player under 14. The winner was twelve-year-old Sophie West, a member of the Southdown East branch and a keen polo player for three years. Her success more than compensated for her disappointment last season, when she had to withdraw right at the start of the championships following a kick in the face by her pony.

On 18th August an old Cowdray tradition continued with the annual invitation match for the Chelsea Bicycle Polo Club, Blues beating Reds 7-6 on the Lawns. Lord Cowdray is a joint-patron of the Bicycle Polo Association of Great Britain, the main areas of the game being round Northampton, Croydon, Warwickshire, Glasgow and, across the Irish Sea, Dublin. The August match at Cowdray Park, starting at lunch-time, makes a pleasant diversion for spectators picnicking before the start of the Brecknock Cup final.

The cup was presented in 1952 by the late Marjorie, Countess of Brecknock, whose son, now Marquess Camden, lead the Pimm's team for so many seasons at Cowdray. The 1991 final saw black-shirted Marabunta defeat yellow-clad Frasers 9-5, the presentation being made by the donor's grand-daughter, Lady Samantha Pratt. It also saw good work from two youngsters: Henry Brett, playing at No. 1 for the victors, and Christian Bearman, a Harrow schoolboy, who played the same position for Frasers.

His father, Garth, was at No. 2 and together they showed that relative newcomers to Cowdray Park can carry on the father-and-son tradition of the Kidds and the Lucases. Suitably, Will Lucas was playing at No. 3 for Frasers.

Henry Brett was on form again on 26th August, when the final of the West Sussex Cup, a favourite low-goal tournament, was played on the River Ground. The West Sussex is one of the oldest trophies at Cowdray Park and its very name symbolises that '18th century privacy' noted by the anonymous write in *The Sphere* over forty years ago. Henry Brett played in his usual position for Red Cell, together with the 3-handicapped David Morley and David Jamison and Peter Hewett (0). Their opponents were Hoyle White, one of a brace of new teams started by Colin Baillieu at Hoyle Farm, Graffham, and named in optimistic emulation of Kerry Packer's Ellerston squads. The previous day, Red Cell had beaten Hoyle Black 4-1$^1/_2$ in the semi-final, and now went on to win the cup 5-3$^1/_2$.

For a time, despite Hoyle White's lack of field goals, it seemed as if Red Cell would be hard-pressed to score. Then Jamison sent a ball between the posts and the game looked up. More than anything, Jamison raised the flag for low-goal polo, a good sign for the country house polo which he is determined to restore to West Sussex.

The rest of the extended season was taken up with the new Autumn Cup league and the Farewell Cup league. By now, the captains and the kings have long departed for France and South America and the yellow standard, bearing the Cowdray family crest, 'in front of a demi-gryphon gules holding between its claws a millstone proper thereon a mill-rind sable, a sun in splendour', no longer floats from the tower of Cowdray House. But the sun in splendour continued to shine on the league matches, and one Farewell Cup match in particular, played between Maidensgrove and Mike and the Mechanics at Ambersham, symbolised the spirit of Cowdray Park. It was a

Chris Bethell

beautifully mild summer evening, the spectators were scattered but devoted and the polo was fun. The absence of Hector Seavill, Maidensgrove's No. 2, meant that the four chukkas were played three-a-side, the opposition, who arrived with a full house, swopping places with each other after chukkas.

In the event, neither side qualified for the final, which was played on 15th September between Marabunta and Red Cell, who won 5-4. It was a close game, and a sad one for Chris Bethell, Red Cell's No. 3, who fell and broke his collarbone a moment or two after the game started. Jonathan Wade was an inspired substitute and the match was for much of the time a tussle between Jonathan and his identical twin, Adrian, playing for Marabunta. If Adrian had managed to score from a penalty in the final seconds, the game would have gone into extra time; as it was, Westerlands vet Patrick Churchward (4) managed to make his team's defeat honourable.

Frasers, 1991: Christian Bearman, Colin Emson, James Lucas and Garth Bearman

There was another honour for a rising star of Cowdray: Alexander Baillieu won the Pimms Trophy for the most improved young player of the season. That day he played at No. 2 for Red Cell and received his award from Marjorie Robinson, widow of Jack Robinson who presented the Farewell Cup over thirty years ago when he ran the Fernhurst team.

Holders reached a final for the first time - and won the new Autumn Cup at Cowdray

Perhaps the most fitting end to the 1991 season came earlier in the afternoon, when Johnnie Kidd's Holders, in purple, beat the blue-shirted Rough Park, $4\frac{1}{2}$-2, in the final of the new Autumn Cup: the first time that Holders had reached a cup final.

The teams are worth recording as having written the first page in a new chapter of polo history at Cowdray Park:

Rough Park	Holders (received $^1/_2$)
1. C.J. Emson (1)	1. C.O. Williams (3)
2. A. Wade (4)	2. J.E.A. Kidd (4)
3. J. Hipwood (8)	3. N. Evans (5)
Bk. T.B.G. Hanlon (2)	Bk. Jack Kidd (2)

We can also be forgiven for repeating the match report, now with others from the season glued safely inside the Cowdray Park scrapbook:

Jack Kidd, the 18-year-old Back for Holders, set the pace in the first chukka, and while several times Holders retained the lead only by their half handicap, they consistently had the lead on Rough Park. In the fourth chukka, Julian Hipwood made a good shot at goal but just not hard enough . . . the ball lay in line only to be missed by his three team-mates in succession. Evans cleared and made a good long shot down the field, allowing Jack Kidd to score at the other end.

The Autumn Cup has been welcomed, particularly by players and others who have known Cowdray Park for a lifetime, and from the spectator's point of view it extends the season agreeably. The prospect of the winter months, bleak enough for non-hunting folk and those who cannot afford to follow the polo trail overseas, is forgotten, if only for an extra fortnight.

Cowdray Park coped admirably, despite the weather and the increased amount of play. Two years earlier, reviewing the 1989 season in the *HPA Year Book,* Alec Harper had written:

The increase in the number of teams and the use of the league system caught us out. Had it not been for fine weather, we would have run out of grounds . . .

and while he was talking of polo in Great Britain generally, one could have been forgiven for applying his comments to prospects for 1991, especially with a new league system for domestic tournaments. Irrigation, which proved a saving grace during the parched 1990 season, was hardly required a year later, yet the season went on with the minimum of postponements.

Johnnie Kidd feels that one fundamental difference in polo now, compared with even twenty years ago, is the lack of time faced by people who enjoy playing, but who also hold down a full-time job.

For serious businessmen, polo is inaccessible, and if you structure a sport so that businessmen are unable to perform, you have a breakdown in the structure of the game. The decision to hold Friday chukkas earlier is a case in point.

It really all comes back to the fact that polo generates its basic activity from a businessman-player writing a cheque. His needs must be catered for, particularly regarding later weekday timing of games and more week-end polo. At the end of the day, a club can only develop if the guy who is writing the cheques has a say in what happens . . .

The future of Young Cowdray is assured, not least by the Pony Club's adoption of the game; but whether, in the 21st century, this means Cowdray Park as a low, or medium, goal centre, or pivot, for the satellite clubs such as David Jamison's Westerlands, remains to be seen. Johnnie Kidd certainly feels that more satellites could be a solution to the frustration felt by many weekend players; while Jamison, although dedicated to recreating 'country house polo' regrets that Cowdray Park, rather than its neighbours, had not taken the initiative in the '80s.

He believes, too, that the English patron will gradually disappear in the future - 'no Englishman can justify £400,000 a year, or whatever it might be' - and that high-goal polo will be sponsored. That, too, remains to be seen: in 1991, for the first time for several years, the Gold Cup at Cowdray Park was unsponsored, a five-year association with Davidoff, who moved to the Royal Berkshire Polo Club, coming to an end the previous season. There are, and will always be, sponsored days: the People Skills match in aid of King Edward VII Hospital; *Country Life*, with the Bentley Drivers' Club, on 2nd June last year, and the Bayerischer Bank on 14th June, among them. No less important is the continuing help from Charles Heidsieck in providing champagne for the winning cups.

Lord Cowdray revived the club with the intention of encouraging the less-wealthy amateur to play, although he was not to foresee the rise of the highly-paid professional, still less perhaps the millionaire patron from overseas. As Michael Pearson notes,

My father has always taken the attitude that polo was a sport he

wanted to keep on an amateur basis but, as time went on, he recognised that professionalism was inevitable. It is still important, however, to keep the club accessible to members, and I think it should remain on that basis as much as possible as we look towards the next century. I am certain that most members, playing and non-playing, would wish Cowdray Park to remain the private club it has always been. The club is healthy and is making a small profit, which will be ploughed back into improved facilities. I very much want to see the traditions continue . . .

It is the traditions, the atmosphere, the lack of what has been termed so aptly the 'glitz and glitter of certain American clubs', which make Cowdray Park so special to those who know it. Hopes for a new ground, next to the Lawns, to be playable at the end of the 1991 season were dashed due to unforeseen drainage problems; but even as we write, the ground, the tenth to be laid out at Cowdray Park, has been relevelled and reseeded and should be in play for late in the 1992 season.

Certainly it will be needed, especially as both Julian Hipwood and Alan Kent hope that the club will soon take up the gauntlet of the short-lived West Sussex Polo Club, at Pulborough, and start and end the season earlier and later.

With good irrigation and good grounds maintenance there is no reason why polo cannot go on longer into the autumn (says Hipwood). There would certainly be terrific support for it, if the number of Cowdray car stickers I see all over the country, really in the most obscure places and at all times of the year, is anything to go by! One thing I would advocate is more money being devoted to the River Ground: it is definitely the best, but last year we began to play there only towards the end of the season . . .

Obviously, there will always be critics, among members and the public, of facilities at Cowdray Park. Last season saw an eminent polo correspondent recording the stands at Cowdray as the worst among the four principal clubs and reporting a regular visitor as condemning catering as 'lousy . . . the indifferent fare . . . is carrying the image of cottage polo a step too far . . . ' Not all those who consume Patrick Kagan's well-known 'brownies' would agree, and there are worse receptacles than plastic mugs from which to drink beer. Indeed, the general consensus of opinion was that it was unfair to compare Cowdray Park with, say, the Royal Berkshire, where the public is welcomed only four days a year and where sponsorship is very much in evidence. From its early days, Cowdray Park has welcomed the public - as Stuart Angell's memories prove - and Arthur Douglas-Nugent recognises the importance of those who watch from the side of the fields opposite the grandstands:

Every sport needs spectators and we encourage the public, if we can call our visitors that, to come to Cowdray Park. They are part of the Cowdray polo tapestry.

Patrick Kagan: sustenance at every match

Joe Plotka and (left) Michael Etherington

Of nearly 800 members at Cowdray Park, 103 were playing members at the end of last season, and of these over fifty were full-time professionals. At the height of the season, as Johnnie Kidd noted, the impact of polo - players, grooms, ponies and visitors - on the Cowdray area is considerable, with shopkeepers, blacksmiths, vets, hotels, saddlers and a host of other businesses benefitting from the influx to Midhurst and neighbourhood. At the same time, Lord Cowdray's devotion to polo has resulted in an extraordinary benefit for the Cowdray Estate. Johnnie Kidd makes the point again:

Compare Cowdray with other country estates and you will see what I mean. Elsewhere, so many estates are dotted with ruined barns, empty cottages and split fields. At Cowdray, although it was never intended to happen, polo has created something of a financial bonanza, with cottages rented during the season, barns and outlying stables repaired and rented by players.

A typical example is the ancient barn at Smokyhouse Lane, on the very edge of the polo grounds at Ambersham. The 1991 season saw Brook

Johnson, patron of Cooch Behar and Ashton Cup winners C.S. Brooks, take a long lease on the derelict barn from the estate and transform the interior with boxes for two dozen ponies. Old tiles and timbers were brought from far and wide to repair the barn and, as a result, Ambersham has a new team on its doorstep.

Indeed, Ambersham can be called a polo village, lacking only a pub: the Old House at Home closed its doors within living memory to become a private house, rented at one stage by the Maharajah of Cooch Behar.

C.S. Brooks is already looking forward to its 1992 attempt to win the Gold Cup, the team unchanged from last season and with Brook Johnson's brother, Tim, forming a low-goal team again based at Ambersham. Kerry Packer will be back with his Ellerston teams, among his players the 'boy wonder' of 1991, Adolfo Cambiaso. Anthony Embiricos and Tramontana will try to retain the cup, and this year the team will include the Prince of Wales who, as he admits in the Foreword, has 'been trying to win the Gold Cup for the past 14 years . . . despite being in the final twice this particular prize has eluded me!'

So, royal ponies will be stabled in the Cowdray area again, recalling those days in the early '50s when the Duke of Edinburgh was a regular player. To see how polo has changed since his days with Mariners and Greyhounds, one has only to look at a cutting from the *Brighton Evening Argus* for 10th May, 1954:

What will the new season offer? Possibly lower playing costs. For Lord Cowdray is trying to bring polo within the pocket of the £10-a-week man . . . It now costs £1 to hire a pony and play one 7½ minute chukka. Although it is doubtful whether any foreign teams will play this season, many top players, including England's Back, Mr John Lakin, will take the field. A low goal league has been created to give young players more experience . . .

Certainly the costs have escalated, the number of players, ponies and matches has increased beyond the wildest dreams of 1954. Foreign teams, at least in recent seasons, have tended to be South American and Australian, and the rise of entries in the Gold Cup leagues has given a distinctly British flavour to the tournament, if only because the teams are based for the duration at the four leading British clubs, Cowdray, Guards, Cirencester and the Royal Berkshire. The professionals, non-existent in

England in 1954, are primarily South American; and yet it cannot be denied that more than one of them - the young Cambiaso is an example - have used Cowdray Park as a springboard to international fame. 'Cowdray Park is the one club at which everyone wants to play' are words that can be translated into any language.

The encouragement given to young players has continued at Cowdray Park and in the scholarships awarded by the Hurlingham Polo Association for youngsters to travel abroad. The medium and low goal tournaments of August and September continue to provide up and coming players with the opportunity to play with, and against, experienced men and, occasionally, women; although whether they risk turning professional depends very much on the economic climate, as Lord Cowdray noted, and on the modern-day equivalent of the £10-a-week man continuing to support the game.

Lavinia Black hopes that Cowdray Park maintains its traditions and 'doesn't cater only for rich people who buy their way into the game', while Richard Guess, welcoming the extended season 'because it helps professionals to earn more money', stresses the importance of keeping the essence of Cowdray unchanged in the future.

Oliver Ellis has no doubts about Cowdray Park in the next century:

The future looks marvellous. Cowdray is the best club, without the shadow of a doubt. At the same time, much is down to how cooperative players and patrons are, and it is every player's responsibility to be as nice as they can to the polo manager - his is often a thankless task . . .

Mollie Tatham remembers an incident not long after her husband, the much-loved 'Bolshie', took over as polo manager. Games were always started punctually and if a patron was not on the field at the correct time, Col Tatham would send in a substitute.

This happened one day and when the patron arrived - during the third chukka, mind you - he was livid. At the end of the match he went up to 'Bolshie' and harangued him in front of everybody. My poor husband had never been spoken to in that way before, even when he was a prisoner-of-war, and his mouth fell open. Anyway, this abuse continued for some time until Alec Harper arrived on the edge of the crowd that had gathered. He went quietly away and fetched John Cowdray, who listened for a moment and then tapped this dreadful patron on the shoulder. It was then the turn of HIS mouth to fall open when Lord Cowdray ordered him and his team off the ground and told them never to return to the club. 'No-one speaks to my polo manager like that,' he said. Poor old 'Bolshie's' jaw dropped even further. John Cowdray really was the best possible boss we could have ever had . . .

Arthur Douglas-Nugent admits that a polo manager must mix tact and determination and wear the skin of a rhinoceros.

My hopes, as we approach the year 2000, would be to keep up standards and provide good grounds, which is really the key to the whole thing. My dream is to continue Cowdray Park as Lord Cowdray would wish it to be played.

Colin Emson, patron of the Frasers team, summed up the thoughts of most players succinctly:

At Cowdray Park we are all Lord Cowdray's guests. Each year we are invited to play, by letter, because Cowdray is still very much a private club: that is part of its inherent charm.

Colin Emson with (right) sons Chase and Henry

Emson, whose 1991 handicap was 1, took up polo as recently as 1980, as a change from club motor racing. He went to Major Hugh Dawnay's Whitfield Court International Polo School, near Waterford, having never even seen a polo match, and was shortly addicted to the game.

I had hunted a but, but I kept falling off. At Whitfield Court there was a gang of us who had never played polo but I was given great encouragement by everyone. A ball was not completely alien to me - I had been a 16 handicap golfer - but I needed a coach back in England and it appeared there was none to be found. Johnnie Kidd suggested that I persuade Terry Hanlon, at Ambersham, to take me on. He was making horses then and his initial reaction was to concentrate on them, rather than teaching players. In the end, I bought six ponies and he agreed to teach me, even though I fell off all the time.

By the winter of 1980 Emson was committed to the game. He took his string of ponies to Bathurst Mews in London - a happy echo from the high days of London polo - and would ride for an hour before work every morning in Hyde Park.

I was so hooked on the game, and on riding properly, that if I went to stay with friends I would take a horse and a trailer with me . . .

In 1981 he was accepted as a chukka member at Cowdray Park and has never looked back. He was part of a team, put together by Terry Hanlon, which won the Jersey Lilies Cup the following year and for two seasons played medium goal polo with a Cowdray Park team, including Patrick Churchward, Charles Pearson and Paul Withers.

I have never played high goal and I never will. I feel, however, that I can make a real contribution to the game up to medium level, but I don't believe that anyone should aim to play in high goal if their handicap is under 3.

Colin Emson is as committed to Cowdray Park as he is to the game, and has 'never felt the need' to consider membership elsewhere.

One thing I do like about Cowdray is the absence of boards on the grounds, although this may be an unpopular attitude to many players. No polo pony is a jumper - boards are dangerous to pony and player - and although the game can seem a bit disjointed if the ball goes out of play because of the lack of boards, we can put up with it! If a match is slowed down a little while a new ball is thrown in, what does it really matter?

Emson was one of a number of players, not all of them from Cowdray Park, subjected to a display of appalling journalistic licence two years ago, when polo came under the scrutiny of a television documentary, *Cutting Edge.* To anyone who played, or who knew anything about the game, the programme could be seen for what it was: a malevolent and misinformed attempt to ridicule the sport. A local television station was to put the record straight with *Game of Kings and Princes* the following season, but many players felt that the 'mud had stuck' because of *Cutting Edge*.

What upset me was the deception of the programme (says Colin Emson). For example, one of Clare Tomlinson's ponies was shown dying on the field and because of the irresponsible editing, Clare and I were made to appear completely heartless. The impression given, deliberately, was that we drive our ponies to death, which is obviously a complete fabrication. Actually, something under fifteen polo ponies die a year, if that, while a far higher number are killed racing. It is, of course, a very emotive subject, but Cutting Edge *used the incident completely out of context. Moreover, some malevolent person invented the story that I, as a merchant banker, had financed the programme for commercial gain.*

Fortunately, polo is not often subjected to television - the game is too fast for one thing -but during the season more accurate match reports are heard, from time to time, on radio. At the moment, however, there appear to be no plans to emulate the 1950s and insert a match commentary at peak listening time on the successor to the old Home Service.

Those who know and love Cowdray Park can take deliberate attacks on the game, or on the club by implication, in their stride. The very lack of commercialism at Cowdray Park is favourable, although Colin Emson foresees some increase on the promotional front as inevitable, even essential, for the future.

Obviously, blatant commercialism must be avoided at all costs; we do not want to reach the stage where the deepest commercial cheque book influences the game. The one thing I love about polo is that, because of the handicap system, someone like me can get into international cross play, as long as you can play well and balance yourself in a team. At Cowdray Park I have been lucky enough to play with some of the best in the world . . .

Anyone who has been to Cowdray Park, in no matter what capacity, surely has one wish: to see a home team win the Gold Cup again. At the time of writing, new ponies are being bought in South America by Alan Kent, although old favourites such as Paul Withers's Archie will be seen again this season on the grounds at Ambersham and on the Lawns and River Ground. The orange shirts will, as ever, be followed closely through-

'My line, my line!' Colin Emson (left) and Mike Rutherford (of Genesis)

out the season, at every level of play; and while Terry Hanlon's wise adage that no-one really ever loses at Cowdray Park is worth remembering, a victory for the home team in the premier polo final in the world would surely provide an ideal basis from which to start the story of Cowdray Park Polo Club in the next century.

No matter if commercialism and more obvious promotionalism is seen in the future - although it will never be blatant in this corner of West Sussex - the fun and the magic of Cowdray Park will remain. One of the authors will long remember his eleventh-hour mission to supply a changing-room, reserved for the Prince of Wales, with soap, towels and lavatory paper, his arrival at the door, arms laden, coinciding with that of the royal player. Such incidents add to the Cowdray tapestry.

One final tribute is in order, from Nicky Evans whose great-grand-

A Golden future

father came to help Harold Cowdray in the early years of the polo, at a time when nobody could possibly foresee the position that the club would eventually attain in international polo.

It is wonderful that Cowdray Park is still John Cowdray's club, one of the things that hasn't changed. At the end of the day, Cowdray Park is unlike anywhere else in polo. The procedure here is John Cowdray: he has this wonderful love for the game and, bar nobody, has done the most for it. Even today he is still contributing his bit . . .

Lord Cowdray: father of English polo

EPILOGUE

This book has spanned almost a century of Cowdray Park and seen it develop, under the present Lord Cowdray and his father, into today's world showcase for polo. A veritable 'polo industry' has evolved around the 40,000 acre estate, with Midhurst becoming the 'polo town' (where people have grown used to the sight of Argentinian Gauchos shopping in Gateways!) which has brought added prosperity to the area. The playing season ends in mid-September, but the industry continues right through the winter. Over 1,000 polo horses, for example, have to be groomed and grazed and brought to the pinnacle of fitness in preparation for next season. This thriving industry is due to the dedication and considerable energy of the present Lord Cowdray, whose name is synonymous with the revival of polo in England.

As a polo venue, there is nowhere quite like Cowdray Park, the ultimate English country estate. The magnificent setting, the sheer spaciousness, the atmosphere, the glamour, the excitement, the spectacle - all play a part in heightening its appeal. And during the period leading up to the Gold Cup, the climax of the season, the tension and excitement escalates. Every July, the most talented players in the world gather to compete for this coveted trophy. Cowdray Park is the players' favourite and constitutes the finest polo club and grounds on their world circuit.

Cowdray Park is also a superb spectator's arena. There is a real feeling of participating and being close to the action, rather than being confined to a distant grandstand. People do of course watch from the stands, but they also tend to move around, chatting, strolling, picnicking and mingling with the players. First time visitors are pleasantly surprised by this friendly informality. It's a social occasion and a day out, for people of all walks of life and of all ages. This delightful 'family' atmosphere is unique and one that Lord Cowdray is most anxious to preserve.The excellent commentaries from Terry Hanlon and, the 'subtle voice of polo', Peter Holman, have made the sport thoroughly comprehensible to all and even more exciting to watch.

The advent of professionalism and commercialism has given polo a much higher profile, which in turn has boosted attendances and attracted sponsors and patrons. It is largely thanks to the present Lord Cowdray that the sport is in such a healthy state today. And despite the increased stakes, polo remains a clean, family sport which is mercifully devoid of the bad behaviour and rowdyism associated with certain others.

Peter Holman: 'subtle voice' of polo

Cowdray Park is reluctantly moving into the 1990s and changes are inevitable. Not big, unsightly changes in the name of progress, but small, subtle changes that are necessary and pleasing to all. Most members want to see some improvements, but none wish to see the fabric and character of the Park unduly altered or spoiled. Changes will therefore be effected with the utmost care and in great taste. And only improvements which are demonstrably needed, not simply for the sake of change and nor with one eye on the competition, will be considered.

Some members have expressed a desire for hard wooden seats to be replaced by something a little softer and kinder to the backside. But if Lord Cowdray, at 82, is willing and able to sit on them for four hours at a time,

The Polo Office, Cowdray Park

perhaps the members can bear to as well! Case rests!

The future looks well for Cowdray Park, too. There is a very long waiting list foı people wishing to become playing members and the club simply cannot cope with them all at present. The scheme to attract more young English players seems to be working admirably.

Michael Pearson has pledged to continue the club in his father's footsteps. Cowdray Park and polo are linked together inexorably for the future - at least until the revised edition of this book in about a century's time . . .

APPENDIX

HPA Handicaps

CH = Current Handicap
FSP = + = Foreign Sponsored Player
PC = X = Pony Club *(under eighteen)*

RH = Recommended Handicap
HGP = Y = High Goal Player
UG = Umpire Grade

SEPTEMBER 23RD, 1991 COWDRAY PARK LIST

NAME	CLUB	CH	RH	FSP	HGP	PC	UG
Aguerre, M.	Cowdray	7		+	Y		A
Ahmad, S.	Cowdray	-1					
Alun-Jones, J.	Cowdray	1					C
Archibald, A.	Cowdray	2			Y		B
Baillieu, D.	Cowdray	-1				X	
Baillieu, A.	Cowdray	1					C
Bearman, C.	Cowdray	0				X	C
Bearman, G.	Cowdray	2					B
Benson, W.	Cowdray	-2				X	
Bethell, C.	Cowdray	4			Y		AB
Black, Mrs L.	Cowdray	1					B
Boher, J.C.	Cowdray	0					
Boyer, Mrs C.	Cowdray	0					
Brett, H.	Cowdray	1				X	C
Brown, M.R.	Cowdray	4			Y		A
Buchanan, A.	Cowdray	3			Y		B
Burnett, C.	Cowdray	-1					
Burnett, S.	Cowdray	1					C
Cambiaso, A.	Cowdray	9		+	Y		
Churchward, W.P.	Cowdray	4					AB
Cooper, T.	Cowdray	-1				X	
Courreges, G.	Cowdray	8		+	Y		A
Cramp, C.	Cowdray	0					C
Cruden, C.V.	Cowdray	1					C
Cruden, P.R.	Cowdray	0					B
Dickson, J.	Cowdray	2					C
Dickson, N.	Cowdray	-2				X	
Dickson, S.	Cowdray	0				X	
Dorignac, G.	Cowdray	6		+	Y		A
Dorman, R.	Cowdray	-2				X	
Douglas-Nugent, A.R.	Cowdray	1					B
Dukes, P.	Cowdray	2			Y		B
Ellis, O.	Cowdray	5			Y		A
Embiricos, A.N.C.	Cowdray	2			Y		B
Emson, C.	Cowdray	-1				X	
Emson, C.J.	Cowdray	1					C
Evans, N.J.	Cowdray	4			Y		AB
Evans, V.	Cowdray	2					B
Ezcurra, T.	Cowdray	6		+	Y		A
Fane, T.	Cowdray	3			Y		B
Farley, G.	Cowdray	1					C
Fattal, A.	Cowdray	1					B
Franklin, M.F.	Cowdray	2					B
Fraser, C. de M.	Cowdray	2					B
Galindo, H.	Cowdray	8		+	Y		A
Gilmore, J.	Cowdray	5		+	Y		AB
Glue, G.	Cowdray	2					B
Glue, M.	Cowdray	5			Y		AB
Gould, I.	Cowdray	5		+			AB
Gracida, C.	Cowdray	10		+	Y		A
Gracida, R.	Cowdray	8		+			A
Graham, R.	Cowdray	4			Y		A
Grossart, J.D.	Cowdray	0					C
Grossart, D.H.	Cowdray	0					C
Guess, R.G.	Cowdray	1			Y		B
Gulab, J.D.	Cowdray	0					C
Hanlon, T.B.G.	Cowdray	1					B
Harvey, Miss A.	Cowdray	0				X	
Healey, W.	Cowdray	3					B
Healy, T.	Cowdray	2					C
Herrera, A.	Cowdray	6		+	Y		A

Sehr Ahmad: rising star

NAME	CLUB	CH	RH	FSP	HGP	PC	UG
Hewett, P.	Cowdray	0					C
Hind, M.	Cowdray	-1				X	
Hipwood, J.	Cowdray	7			Y		A
Hissom, R.	Cowdray	2			Y		B
Hobden, E.	Cowdray	1					C
Jamison, D.L.	Cowdray	3			Y		AB
Johnson, C.B.	Cowdray	2			Y		B
Johnson, C.D.	Cowdray	1					B
Kent, A.J.	Cowdray	7			Y		A
Kidd, J.	Cowdray	2				X	C
Kidd, J.E.A.	Cowdray	3			Y		AB
Laugher, W.	Cowdray	-1				X	
Law, V.	Cowdray	0					
Lawson, G.C.H.	Cowdray	1					C
Lawson J.	Cowdray	0					
Leathers, N.	Cowdray	-2				X	
Leech, A.	Cowdray	0				X	
Lucas, J.C.L.	Cowdray	5			Y		A
Lucas, W.	Cowdray	6			Y		A
Macaire, L.	Cowdray	8		+	Y		A
Mackenzie, S.	Cowdray	8		+	Y		A
MacKenzie-Hill, M.	Cowdray	2			Y		B
Manoukian, V.	Cowdray	-1					
Mason, Lt Cdr R.	Cowdray	2					B
McLean, N.	Cowdray	1					C
Mejia, C.	Cowdray	0					C
Milford Haven, The Marquess of	Cowdray	2			Y		B
Morley, D.S.	Cowdray	3					AB
O'Grady, H.	Cowdray	0				X	
Olazabal, M.	Cowdray	1			Y		
Olazabal, D.	Cowdray	2			Y		
Omar, R.	Cowdray	0					C
Packer, J.	Cowdray	2			Y		C
Packer, K.P.	Cowdray	1			Y		C
Pearson, The Hon C.A.	Cowdray	2			Y		B
Pieres, A.	Cowdray	10		+	Y		A
Pieres, G.	Cowdray	10		+	Y		A
Rhodes, P.M.	Cowdray	1					C
Rinehart, O.	Cowdray	9		+	Y		A
Roberts, C.R.	Cowdray	1					C
Roberts, I.P.	Cowdray	0					C
Roberts, W.S.	Cowdray	3			Y		B
Roddick, G.	Cowdray	1					C
Rutherford, M.	Cowdray	0					C
Santos, J.	Cowdray	4		+			B
Seavill, A.	Cowdray	5			Y		A
Seavill, C.A.S.	Cowdray	4					AB
Seavill, C. Snr.	Cowdray	0					C
Seavill, H.	Cowdray	2					B
Secunda, M.	Cowdray	0				X	
Sharp, J.R.	Cowdray	0					
Shepherd, O.	Cowdray	-2				X	
Shepherd, R.	Cowdray	-1				X	
Simonds, G.D. (Sam)	Cowdray	1					C
Snow, A.	Cowdray	8		+	Y		A
Sosa, O.	Cowdray	8		+	Y		A
Stakemire, T.	Cowdray	3					AB
Stevens, H.C.	Cowdray	1					B
Szell, B.	Cowdray	-2				X	
Tanoira, G.	Cowdray	9		+	Y		A
Tari, B.	Cowdray	3			Y		
Tari, G.	Cowdray	3			Y		
Vivian Smith, C.V.	Cowdray	1					C
Wade, A.	Cowdray	4			Y		AB
Wade, J.	Cowdray	4			Y		AB
Wade, J.C.	Cowdray	0					C
White, R.	Cowdray	0					C
Williams, C.O.	Cowdray	3					B
Williams, S.	Cowdray	3					C
Willoughby, M.	Cowdray	1					B
Withers, P.M.	Cowdray	6			Y		A
Yeoman, J.F.	Cowdray	1			Y		B
Zavaletta, C.	Cowdray	8		+	Y		A

Into the future: the new ground under way

INDEX

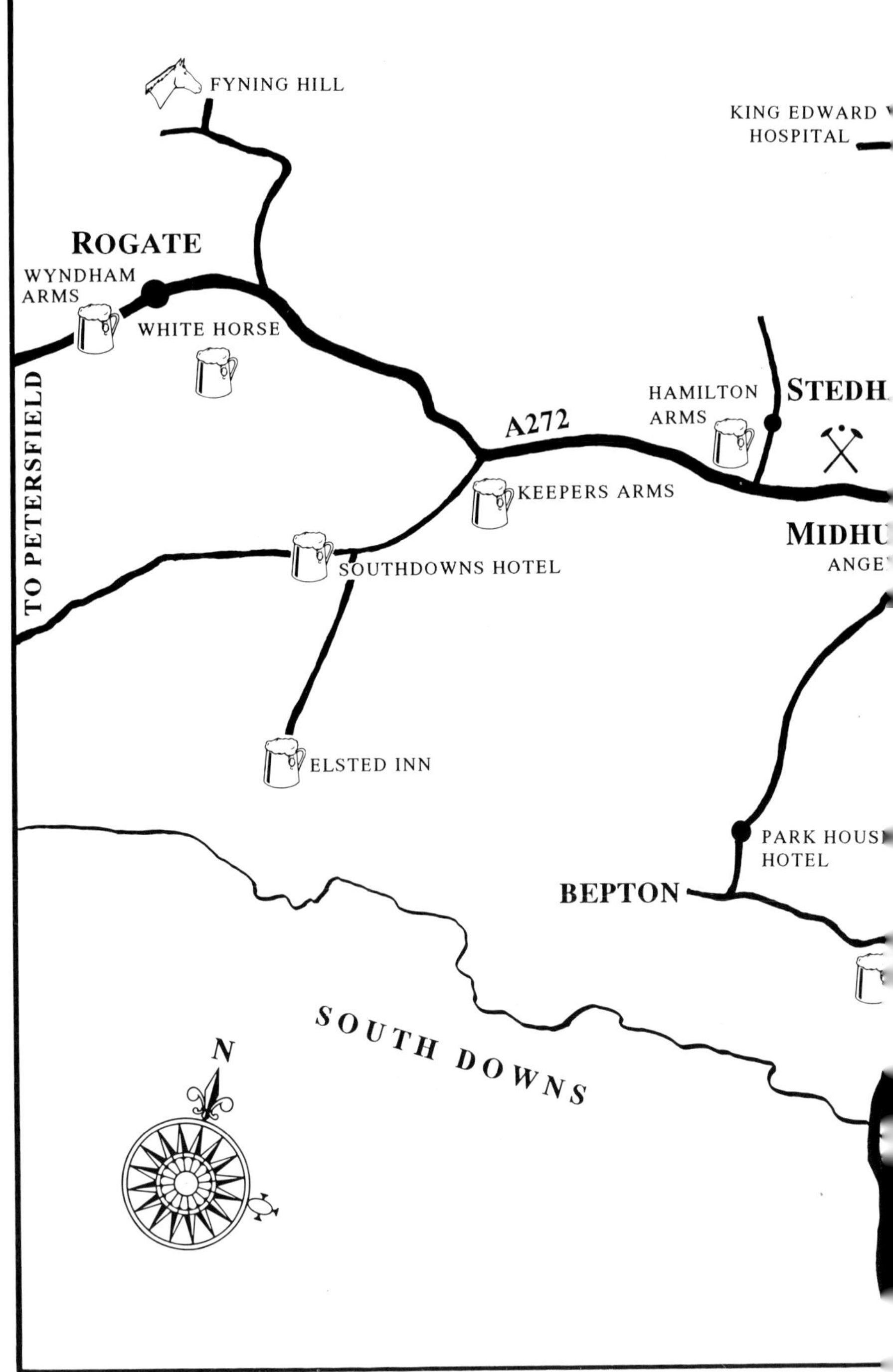
FYNING HILL
KING EDWARD
HOSPITAL
ROGATE
WYNDHAM
ARMS
WHITE HORSE
TO PETERSFIELD
A272
HAMILTON
ARMS
KEEPERS ARMS
SOUTHDOWNS HOTEL
ELSTED INN
PARK HOUSE
HOTEL
BEPTON
SOUTH DOWNS
N